Designing Curriculum

John D. McNeil
University of California, Los Angeles

DESIGNING CURRICULUM
Self-Instructional Modules

LITTLE, BROWN AND COMPANY
Boston Toronto

Copyright © 1976 by Little, Brown and Company (Inc.)

All rights reserved.
No part of this book may be reproduced in any form or by any electronic or mechanical means including information storage and retrieval systems without permission in writing from the publisher, except by a reviewer who may quote brief passages in a review.

Library of Congress Catalog Card No. 76-12792

First printing

Published simultaneously in Canada
by Little, Brown & Company (Canada) Limited

Printed in the United States of America

Preface

When people grow impatient with a curriculum handed down by others, they require a different emphasis — one that features local participation in curriculum-making. These four modules are written for a wide range of participants: teachers, administrators, parents — all who are interested in how best to decide *what* should be taught particular learners, to develop the most appropriate learning activities, and to evaluate the effectiveness of instructional materials, courses, and programs.

These modules are self-instructional. They are not monographs dealing with small corners of curriculum, nor are they attempts to place all facts and theories of curriculum-making into a coherent system. As practical text material, they draw from a number of sources and represent an aim at brevity and simplicity of teaching.

A theorist may consider curriculum as a series of intended outcomes, valued learning experiences, or the way an individual learner interprets what happens in school. Practitioners, too, have different conceptions. Some believe that certain experiences, learning opportunities, or kinds of content are good in and of themselves and that all children should have them. Others tend to prize particular learner performances and to regard content and experiences as mere means to be appraised. Hence, the modules in this book have been designed to serve several orientations.

The first module focuses on procedures for helping practitioners in instructional and product development. In the second and third modules, we shall deal with curriculum as a series of intended outcomes and with the processes for formulating these ends. In the fourth module, we shall clarify the processes of evaluation in designing, improving, and selecting among curricula. All of the modules stop short at the point where planning becomes teaching. They do not include instructions for carrying out curriculum plans in the teacher-student interactive phases. Although the modules do not include everything that ought to be known about curriculum-making, each module deals with six or seven essential competencies in curriculum-making. The twenty-seven competencies are essential in two ways: (1) They serve as a springboard to learning more about curriculum-making. Possession of these initial competencies will allow one to be a better student of curriculum — that is, to be familiar with useful concepts and fruitful questions. (2) They enable one to make more intelligent decisions about what and how to teach.

In addition to the competencies, the modules offer other helpful material for curriculum planners. Many propositions such as means–ends relations in curricular thought are presented to help one understand the nature of inquiry and the methods used in curriculum-making.

The modules can be adapted to fit different needs. They are excellent supplements to a formal course in curriculum and instruction. They can be given at different times to accommodate the organization of the course. Students who work through the modules will be prepared for more significant learning experiences with an instructor; they will have added a "learning set" and orientation as well as basic concepts to their repertoire. Since the modules do not, however, require an instructor, they can be used as (1) the basis for a special interest study within an educational program, (2) a means for self-improvement and professional growth in independent study, or (3) a component in a program for staff development or in-service education. The modules were tried out and found to be valuable by students of education including teachers, administrators, and parents, who represented a range of interests and educational levels.

Within the modules are introductions, statements of competencies or objectives, background information necessary for each competency, examples, and exercises followed by answers and feedback. Achievement occurs through brief didactic presentations and opportunities for the user to apply what is read and to receive further explanation, if wanted, in order to clarify the content.

Contents

Module 1   *The Design and Selection of Learning Activities*   1

Intrinsic Qualities — A Criterion for Judging Learning Activities   5

Instrumental Values — A Second Criterion for Judging Learning Activities   9

Individualization — A Third Criterion for Judging Learning Activities   23

Efficiency — A Fourth Criterion for Judging Learning Activities   33

Summary   41

Module 2   *Deriving Objectives*   43

Levels of Decision-Making Regarding Outcomes   47

Deriving Objectives from Studies of the Learners   51

The Community as a Source of Objectives   57

Deriving Objectives from Subject Specialists   63

Summary   71

Module 3   *Selecting among Educational Objectives — Defensible Choices*   73

The Needs Assessment Approach to Selecting Educational Objectives   79

Philosophical Models   85

Psychological Models for Deciding What to Teach   93

Summary   101

Module 4   *Evaluating the Effectiveness of the Curriculum*   105

Instruments and Situations   109

Design and Decisions   129

Summary   137

Module 1
THE DESIGN AND SELECTION OF LEARNING ACTIVITIES

Learning activities—sometimes called learning opportunities, learning experiences, or instructional interventions—are the essence of education. As one wag said, "Aims and objectives are the menu, learning activities are the meal." Field trips, dramatizations, textbooks, films, debates, experiments, games, and the like can be the means by which learners both experience valued aspects of life and acquire desirable concepts, skills, and attitudes.

Learning activities vary in form and duration, and in other ways, such as the degree to which they involve real-world situations as opposed to imaginary or academic ones. All learning activities, however, are meant to effect some change in the learner, or to exemplify a cultural value. Many do both.

Anyone who desires to shape or influence the learning of others should find it helpful to be able to apply the principles for designing and selecting activities. This includes teachers and parents who must plan the activities that they will later carry out with their learners; administrators; board members; members of curriculum textbook committees; and others who must justify their decisions regarding the activities which they purchase or authorize in schools. Not all school leaders will need to apply those principles to actually create instructional materials; however, they must be able to judge the adequacy of the activities used in their schools. Further, those who would improve the effectiveness of present activities must be able to identify the presence or absence of certain instructional variables, principles, or conditions associated with successful activities.

OBJECTIVES OF THIS MODULE

Hence, this module was prepared to help the user achieve the following competencies necessary for designing and selecting learning activities:

4 — THE DESIGN AND SELECTION OF LEARNING ACTIVITIES

1. Given descriptions of learning activities or actual instructional products, the user will be able to identify those which satisfy essential criteria. The essential criteria include:
   a. intrinsic features
   b. instrumental values
   c. individualization
   d. efficiency
   (three *i*'s and an *e*)
2. The user will be able to illustrate principles of task analysis and appropriate practice (both equivalent and analogous).
3. On examining learning activities, the user will be able to identify instances of the following techniques for helping learners attend to relevant cues:
   a. organizers
   b. objectives
   c. prompts
   d. contiguity
   e. feedback
4. Given learners with different levels of ability, the user will be able to select from among several activities the one that is most appropriate for each learner.
5. The user will be able to create learning activities that appeal through:
   a. manipulation
   b. incongruity
   c. involvement of a "significant other"
   d. confluence
6. Given learners with particular cultural predispositions (such as field sensitivity) and other personality differences (such as anxiety), the user will be able to select the activities most likely to be satisfying for each learner.
7. Given several different activities, the user will be able to identify those which are consistent with the principles of economy, variation, and simplicity.

Intrinsic Qualities— A Criterion for Judging Learning Activities

Activities in an educational setting differ from many of the activities found in life at large. On the one hand, educational activities are purposive. Often they are chosen because they are *not* found in naturalistic settings—because they can help learners achieve what otherwise would not be possible. On the other hand, educational activities must reflect what the culture deems desirable. Activities for a Fagen's school, such as setting up a "pigeon drop," must not be selected.

Chief among the intrinsic qualities that should be present in all learning opportunities for the American society is respect for the preciousness or integrity of the human being. The premise that the learner is important as an individual, that his well-being is vital in itself, is held as a legal right and as education's moral commitment. The learner is then regarded as an end, rather than a means. Hence learning activities should be planned so that individual differences are respected and so learners have maximum freedom, consistent with the general welfare, to develop as they desire.

6 — THE DESIGN AND SELECTION OF LEARNING ACTIVITIES

Exercise 1 *Recognizing instances consistent with human rights*

Place a check mark alongside each description of an activity in which concern for human rights is an intrinsic quality.

_____ 1. The learner is allowed to make an informed choice in carrying out the activity but must reflect on the consequences of the choice.

_____ 2. Completion of the activity can be accomplished by learners of different levels of ability.

_____ 3. The activity requires the learner to examine issues ignored by the mass media.

_____ 4. The activity allows for the learner to share in its planning.

_____ 5. The activity denies the learner the risk of failure — success is ensured.

_____ 6. The learner is required to exert effort.

_____ 7. The activity will strike students as relevant to the world they know — to their expressed purposes.

_____ 8. Completion of the activity depends on access to data not available to all.

_____ 9. The activity provides for a learner's expression of personal ideas.

_____ 10. The activity takes into account the learner's cultural values.

Answers

Number 8 should not have been checked. This activity does not provide for equality of opportunity. Also, many scholars of freedom would not check number 5 on the grounds that the right to fail – to take risks – is essential to the fullness of a human being. All other instances treat the individual as precious and as an end, not as an instrument.

Exercise 2 *Generating intrinsic qualities*

Try now to think of other qualities whose very presence indicates that an activity is worthwhile. You may wish to think of the characteristics present in natural environments that you consider inspirational. Perhaps you will prize aesthetic values, such as patterns, contrasts, balance, or unity, or you might consider the characteristics of great poets, scientists, and statesmen. You might want to consider the values you would use in making such choices as: Peter Pan versus Superman; *Hamlet* versus *Kojak*; the art gallery versus the shooting gallery. Try reflecting on the activities or works that have been influential in developing civilization, those which have delighted for generations, or those which deal with personal and universal concerns and allow for many interpretations. Then decide if they have any features in common. Maybe you can arrive at qualities best by thinking about critical events (past or present) in which all persons should share. List below the qualities you tend to prize as good in themselves.

Answers

Each quality listed should be of intrinsic value, not a characteristic that must be appraised or valued for its contribution to something else.

8 – THE DESIGN AND SELECTION OF LEARNING ACTIVITIES

TO INFLUENCE VERSUS TO SHAPE

Activities are often selected on the basis of an intrinsic quality when one wants to *influence* rather than *shape*. To influence is to present what one thinks is an activity from which learners may develop in many desirable but unspecified ways. For instance, a teacher who plans for children to go to the tide pools may select this trip without predetermined objectives or without specifying in advance the outcome that will signify success. He or she believes that the tide pools are a good learning opportunity; perhaps a chance to learn something related to cooperation, healthy environment, ethics, and countless other worths, depending on what the learner himself develops from the "rich exposure." To shape, however, is to present activities and to structure them so that learners achieve prespecified objectives and they come away from the activity with a specific attitude, understanding, or skill. When shaping, one tends less to focus on the intrinsic quality of the activity than to look for its instrumental value.

Instrumental Values — A Second Criterion for Judging Learning Activities

Most learning activities are judged "good" when they "work." That is to say, a learning activity must lead to the attainment of an instructional objective. According to this criterion, when an activity does not result in some expected or desired outcome—when the learners do not acquire the kind of skills, attitudes, or knowledge sought through the activity—then the activity is "invalid." In short, activities are perceived as means and the objective as their end. Unlike the criterion of intrinsic worth, the criterion of instrumental values demands evidence that the activity is creating desirable responses in the learner. There is no inherent value in the activity itself. As Dewey said, "It is no reflection upon the nutritive quality of beefsteak that it is not fed to infants." According to this criterion, there is no educational value in the abstract. This criterion means that there must be both an objective and an activity. One can look at an activity and then infer the objective that should follow, or one can start with an objective and then plan an activity that is likely to promote its attainment.

Are there any guidelines that are useful in selecting learning activities that work? What is known about designing learning activities that maximize attainment of objectives?

We will examine three principles of learning (rules of action), which when followed in the design of learning activities enhance achievement. Two of these, the principles of *task analysis* and *appropriate practice*, stem from the *law of identical elements*—a conclusion derived from the studies of Thorndike. Briefly, this law states that in order for an activity to be effective, it must contain elements identical to the objective. "To take a concrete example, improvement in addition will alter one's ability in multiplication because addition is absolutely identical with a part of multiplication."[1] What we learn tends to be quite specific to the particular learning situation and to those exactly like it. When we expect learners to transfer what they learn to a broad range of situations, we must give them specific opportunities to practice such transfer.

THE PRINCIPLE OF TASK ANALYSIS

This principle recommends focusing on an objective (task) and then determining what one would have to know or be able to do in order to perform the task (achieve the objective). A list of prerequisite skills or knowledge constitutes a task analysis.

By way of example, consider what is necessary before a person can drive an automobile in your local community. An objective for this task might include specifications such as the kind of auto to be driven and the kind of driving situation. Probably the list of minimal prerequisites would include knowledge of rules of the road and the ability to start, reverse, and stop the car, to operate the brakes (and the clutch and gear shift in some cases), to interpret various instruments indicating oil pressure and gas, and to operate such equipment as lights and windshield wipers.

Notice that this sample analysis does not include numerous

1. Edward Lee Thorndike, *The Psychology of Learning,* Vol. 2 of *Educational Psychology* (New York: Teachers College, Columbia University, 1913), p. 358.

"nice to know" items associated with advanced tasks of automobile operation and maintenance, such as the ability to adjust the carburetor, or change the oil. Neither does the analysis specify those many prerequisites that are usually already within the repertoire of most learners, the ability to hear, see, and interpret signs and signals, the ability to distinguish left from right. The point of the example is to show that even the most commonly learned tasks involve a number of prerequisites that must be taught and that successful achievement depends on whether or not each of the prerequisites is learned.

Our assumption is that learning activities will be better designed if we first analyze the task. Indeed, after making such an analysis, the designer may decide that many more activities are needed than first thought and that an activity involving all the complexities of the objective must be deferred until the prerequisites are taught. It is very possible that through a task analysis one ends up designing separate activities for prerequisites instead of a simple activity equivalent to the original objective.

Inasmuch as it is of major importance that designers be able to generate prerequisites to achievement of objectives, the following exercise will offer practice in doing so.

Exercise 3 *Preparing a task analysis*

List at least three prerequisites to the five-year-old's task of learning to tie shoelaces.

12 — THE DESIGN AND SELECTION OF LEARNING ACTIVITIES

Answers

Your answer should have listed items logically related to the task or to the child's ability to understand the instruction for teaching the task. You should *not* have listed something that one who has achieved the objective cannot do, for example, counting the number of eyelets. You might have listed such items as:

1. Knowing concepts "under-over," "in-out," "around," "left-right," "tight."
2. Showing psychomotor ability in holding, turning, pulling, guiding fine material.
3. Having a desire to learn to tie shoes, being enthusiastic about participating in the task, and being confident in ability to succeed.

Perhaps you have noticed that each of the categories involves a different kind of learning—cognitive, psychomotor, affective. An argument for task analysis is that it identifies prerequisites that require different conditions of learning.

Exercise 4 *Analyzing prerequisites to a task*

State in the following space a learning task or objective of interest to you.

Now list at least three prerequisites to the above objective.

Answers

Your answer should indicate something that normally would preclude attaining the objective, something logically necessary, and nothing that one who has achieved the objective *cannot* do.

THE PRINCIPLE OF APPROPRIATE PRACTICE

One learns what one does—the acts that are performed, the thoughts and feelings that are experienced, the words that are spoken. Maybe you think this is self-evident, but much current practice diverges from this single principle. For example, we often offer activities in which pupils recall and identify words and principles when we really want them to put the statements into practice.

There is a certain tension between the principle of appropriate practice and the criterion of intrinsic qualities. When one focuses on activities that represent the highest standards of life (old-timers used to call it the principle of purity), pupils do not have the opportunity to learn how to interpret and deal with the ugly aspects of life. Many religious schools, for instance, have found it necessary to give pupils practice in reacting to a range of material previously excluded—for example, drugs, abortion. They know, too, that practice with only idealistic views of the world and ignoring controversial issues does not inoculate against future influences in the real world.

I mention this here because "ban the book" is back. In one extreme case, strikes, violence, and death threats followed a school board's selection of learning activities featuring the writings of Allen Ginsberg, Eldridge Cleaver, and others. The selection of these materials did not meet the community's criterion for intrinsic qualities. Protesters were particularly angry about: (1) stories with words like these: "A tall, red-headed chick. She had been mainly a whore, actually with expensive johns, who would pay her a hundred dollars a shot. And she was a lively chick who took a lot of pot."[2] (2) books that introduced the concept of myth, in which illustrations from the Bible were labeled as fable and legend; (3) multicultural works that seemingly argued for unpopular practices such as polygamy. The books might, however, have been used to enhance the values of protesters, teachers, and board alike. Indeed, analysis of protesters' concern reveals that they were as much or more concerned about the consequences of pupils' use of the material as about the material itself. They feared that pupils would believe that God and the Bible are myths, be estranged from the closeness of their families, be more violent, and be less supportive of the nation.

Neither side considered what could be added to the presentation of these materials so that they would serve the moral, political, and social advancement of pupils. Unfortunately, the professional staff had limited vision regarding the potential of the books, seeing them chiefly as vehicles for getting the children to write and use their imaginations.

Exercise 5   *Recognizing activities that offer practice equivalent to the level of behavior called for by the objective*

Look at the following three objectives with their sets of learning activities. In the blank provided, write the letter of the activity in each set that gives the learners an opportunity to practice learning identical to that defined by its objective.

---

2. Reported by Robert C. Small, Jr., College of Education, Virginia Polytechnic Institute and State University, in "Textbooks and Schools," a paper presented at the American Educational Studies Convention, San Francisco, California, 1975.

Objective 1. When orally given plural nouns, pupils will be able to write the correct spelling of the plural form.

a. The pupil orally spells the words "going," "house," "family," "man."
b. The pupil states the rule governing formation of plurals for nouns ending in _y_.
c. The pupil selects the words that are not spelled correctly: boxs, dishes, dolles.
d. The pupil writes the word corresponding to "ladies," horses," "feet."

Objective 2. Given quadratic equations, the students will solve them.

a. The teacher demonstrates the solving of quadratic equations.
b. The students provide solutions to quadratic equations.
c. The students propose quadratic equations needing solutions.
d. The students look at examples showing how equations were solved.

Objective 3. Given paragraphs never seen before, learners will be able to summarize what is read.

a. The students read a paragraph and then list the important points made by the author.
b. After reading a paragraph, the students look at a summary of the paragraph and state what is missing.
c. The students read a paragraph, and then list the facts in one column and the opinions in another.
d. After reading a paragraph, the students look at a summary and tell how the summary distorts the meaning of the paragraph.

16 – THE DESIGN AND SELECTION OF LEARNING ACTIVITIES

Answers

1. *d* Only *d* is identical to the objective, writing and spelling of plural nouns. This is not to say that *c* might not contribute to the objective. However, it is not identical.
2. *b* All other options are asking for something other than the learner's solving of problems, for example, the identifying of problems.
3. *a* Notice that the objective does not say that the summary must be written. Identical practice often requires attending to the mode of response as well as to the basic behavior desired (in this case, summarizing) and to the kind of situation demanding that response (here, a paragraph).

LEVELS OF BEHAVIOR

In examining learning opportunities such as textbooks and films, it is useful to classify the levels of behavior demanded of learners.

These three levels of behavior, from lowest to highest, are common:

1. *Knowledge* recall of specific facts or principles. Examples: What proportion of the United States population is living on farms? Which statement below best summarizes Ohm's Law?
2. *Comprehension* recognition of other instances of the principle or term and interpretation of the material read or heard. Example: Look at this new political cartoon and then state the message it conveys.
3. *Application* using concepts or principles in new situations. Example: Predict the direction and amount of change in rate and depth of breath, perspiration, temperature of air which will result from the following experiment.

Exercise 6 *Classifying objectives on three levels of behavior*

Examine the activities numbered below and then indicate at left the highest level of behavior demanded in each.

a. knowledge   b. comprehension   c. application

_____ 1. Employing trigonometry to measure the height of a building never seen before

_____ 2. Describing the structure and organization of Congress

_____ 3. Recognizing examples of propaganda techniques in advertising

_____ 4. Interpreting graphs and diagrams

_____ 5. Influencing others by using psychological principles such as *reinforcement*

_____ 6. Using phonics to decode new words

_____ 7. Finding artistic features (such as hard lines or negative space) in objects

_____ 8. Stating information and principles of importance to health

Answers

1. *c* (*application*) The activity calls for applying a concept in a new instance.
2. *a* (*knowledge*) The student is asked to recall information.
3. *b* (*comprehension*) The activity demands recognition of a concept.
4. *b* (*comprehension*) Interpretation takes place.
5. *c* (*application*) The knowledge is applied in a complex setting.

6. c *(application)* The knowledge is applied in a complex setting.
7. b *(comprehension)* There is recognition of an attribute or concept.
8. a *(knowledge)* There is recall.

The above exercise should help you to see different levels of behavior in activities. However, it should be made clear that additional levels are possible. You may find it helpful to see if activities provide for analysis of relationships, synthesis of elements to form a new pattern or whole, and evaluation in which the learner makes judgments about the value of material and method for a given purpose.

Ability to identify levels of behavior is helpful in applying the principles of both task analysis and appropriate practice. With respect to task analysis, successful application often depends on comprehension, and comprehension, in turn, frequently depends on knowledge or recall of particular facts. Hence, prerequisites are revealed by attending to a hierarchy of levels. Similarly, an activity meets the criterion for appropriate practice only when the practice is at the level of behavior specified by the objective. For example, practice in recalling a rule of grammar is not sufficient to attain the objective of being able to apply the rule in writing a sentence.

THE PRINCIPLE OF ATTENDING TO RELEVANT CUES

Our third rule of action for designing learning activities is to get pupils to attend to relevant cues or to notice crucial features in an activity. When pupils pay attention to the wrong cues, objectives are seldom reached. For example, vivid pictures, exciting motivational approaches, and opportunities to listen to others reading (all of which are commonly found in the young child's beginning activities for learning to read) often distract the child from attending to the visual cues so necessary in learning to distinguish one word from another.

Associated with focused attention are notions about advanced organizers, objectives, contiguity, prompting, and confirming or providing for knowledge of results.

1. *Organizers* Some have tried to improve cueing through the use of *advanced organizers* — nontechnical overviews or outlines of what is to be learned, in which the nonessentials are ignored. However, it is more difficult to convey or preview what is to come when an abstract idea is to be presented. Hence, *descriptions* of concrete models of the abstract ideas are often used, even though the models involve extraneous features.

    It remains unclear whether the organizer must always precede the activity. Many studies have shown that placing an organizer after an activity can facilitate learning.

2. *Questions* Provisions for questions in the activity are very important in cueing learners. Questions at the beginning, during, or at the end of an activity help shape and elicit relevant responses. Notice that here we are considering questions as a means of directing the learners' attention rather than as a means of arousing interest and motivation.

3. *Objectives* Activities that provide specific objectives for the learners are thought to provide direction and assist in discriminating between relevant and incidental content. Perhaps, too, objectives can serve as advance organizers, facilitating the learner's integration of information by providing a general structure to the content.

4. *Prompts* Prompting is another way to help learners both attend to the "right" stimuli and make the right response. A prompt is a hint to help a student respond correctly. Attention can be drawn to particular items through color, italics, movement, loudness of sounds, sharpness of image, and texture. Verbal prompts such as incomplete rhymes, metaphors, and thematic sentences can help the learner attend to right responses. Care should be taken, however, that the learner attend to the critical cue, not rely on the prompt alone in making the response.

5. *Contiguity* When two objects, events, or concepts are experienced together (contiguously), they come to be associated with each other. Therefore, designers of materials often lead a learner to attend to something new by presenting it with something to which the learner already attends; for example, in one readiness book, a picture of a popular cartoon figure is shown at the beginning of each activity engaging in the very task to which pupils must attend. Children associate pictures of objects when they are shown in *relation* to one another and not just paired. In other words, one should show a picture of a child making the letter *A* rather than a picture of a child and a picture of the letter *A*.

6. *Feedback* Feedback is information given to the learners concerning their performance. It provides cues and guidance that assist in the shaping of learning. An activity that provides for letting learners know if their responses are right or wrong helps somewhat, but feedback indicating what must be done to make the incorrect response right is better. By way of example, an activity can be structured so that after a twenty-minute lecture: (1) three essay questions are distributed (requiring students to use and apply what was contained in the

lecture); (2) there is provision for (a) ten minutes in which students write their answers and (b) fifteen minutes in small "buzz" groups to discuss, compare, and check answers using text and notes; and (3) there is allowance for a second general session in which each group can present its unresolved questions.

Exercise 7 *Identifying techniques for promoting relevant attention*

Read each activity and indicate which of the following techniques is best exemplified by each:

a. organizer b. feedback c. questions
d. contiguity e. prompt f. objective

_____ 1. A sample of the kind of product expected from an activity is shown initially.

_____ 2. Provision is made to animate one element in the activity.

_____ 3. An unfamiliar practice or product is presented together with a familiar concept, such as death, signified by a skull and crossbones.

_____ 4. A textbook features chemically impregnated inks which change color when moistened, thereby evaluating the responses made.

_____ 5. Pupils in attending a foreign movie are to record the expressions used in the film that are instances of subjunctive, preterite, and future tenses.

_____ 6. Activities for teaching pupils to read a slide rule scale include alternated short segments of filmed demonstration and practice.

22 — THE DESIGN AND SELECTION OF LEARNING ACTIVITIES

_____ 7. To get pupils to arrive at a conclusion regarding a course of action, an analogy is drawn.

_____ 8. All the common properties in sets of items are marked in a particular way.

Answers

1. a (*organizer*) An example of what is to be learned is provided.
2. e (*prompt*) One is prompted by the association to look at the relevant stimulus. Presumably this was the desired response.
3. d (*contiguity*) The idea of death should be related to the new product.
4. b (*feedback*) There is knowledge of results.
5. a (*organizer*) The assignment specifies what is to be observed.
6. a (*organizer*) Although the film is an organizer, it could also serve as a prompt.
7. e (*prompt*) The analogy is a hint as to what is wanted.
8. e (*prompt*) Presumably the markings prompt attention to the critical feature — but it would be better if learners also had to specify in what way objects with given markings were alike.

Individualization — A Third Criterion for Judging Learning Activities

Individualization requires attending to two kinds of data about the learners who are to engage in the activity. Both kinds are necessary if one believes that the individual learner is the constant in the educational equation, not the activity itself nor the objective it is to promote. One needs an indication that the learner has the background necessary for successful participation in the activity, and one should have reasons for believing that the learner will find the activity satisfying or rewarding.

A well-intended group of planners in a "Higher Horizons" program thought it would be good to take poor children from slum neighborhoods and expose them to the great cultural resources of the city — museums, concerts, and the like. These planners were dismayed to find that the pupils were unable to notice what was present to be seen and heard. Instead of gaining from the experiences, the children expressed their distaste by slashing and marking the pictures and engaging in other negative acts. The trouble was, of course, that the planners had not made a list of the prerequisites that would be necessary before one could participate in the activity. They had not provided for equipping the children with these prerequisites before forcing the activity upon them. On

24 — THE DESIGN AND SELECTION OF LEARNING ACTIVITIES

page 10, the principle of task analysis was presented as a way of enhancing the instrumental value of an activity. Now, however, the same principle is mentioned as a useful guide to *individualization*. Armed with a task analysis and a simple measure for each prerequisite, the planners can determine whether interested learners lack all, some, or none of the prerequisites before participating.

The practice of including a pretest that will indicate the prerequisites shown in a task analysis is one example of how to determine that the proposed activity is within the range of possibility for the learner. A less precise but important way to judge whether a learner would be likely to perform well in an activity is to reflect on the child's background and level of conduct and compare this information with that required by the activity.

Exercise 8 *Identifying activities that are consistent with learning ability*

Look at each description of a learner and then indicate which of two activities is more appropriate for that learner.

_____ 1. The learner comprehends orally but has difficulty deriving inferences from passages.
   a. documentary film and discussion
   b. textbook and written assignment

_____ 2. A primary school child should learn the meaning of interdependence.
   a. visiting and describing the assembly line of a local factory
   b. describing roles taken in a class project

_____ 3. An aged learner has a poor memory for facts.
   a. writing a paper with benefit of notes and resource materials
   b. writing a paper without notes and resource materials

_____ 4. The pupil hasn't heard of the Dewey Decimal System and is unfamiliar with guides to periodicals.
   a. an oral report using information found in the library
   b. a written report based on an interview

_____ 5. The student lacks the technical vocabulary associated with a principle of physics.
   a. reading a chapter in a physics textbook involving the principle
   b. viewing a demonstration of the principle

_____ 6. A student who has a short attention span needs to learn the concept that the brain is the center of coordination.
   a. writing names with the hand pupil does not regularly use, picking up marbles with chopsticks, and finding the patterns of fifty numbers on a page
   b. getting information from a variety of sources such as an interview with a physiologist, reading, and a field trip to a neuropsychiatric clinic

_____ 7. A child who comes from an isolated reservation needs encouragement to develop good novel ideas.
   a. listing everything he or she might find in a kitchen
   b. listing everything he or she might find in a music store

_____ 8. The child is shy.
   a. choral singing
   b. solo singing

Answers

1. *a* Such an oral presentation is consistent with the ability of the learner. This example illustrates a limitation, however. By circumventing a difficulty, the child may achieve an intended objective without overcoming the deficit.

2. *b* This activity is more in keeping with experiences of the young child. Activity *a* is too complex.
3. *a* Remember that in this exercise one is to adapt the activity to a particular status, not change that status. Presumably, the activity of writing the paper serves an objective other than development of memory or recall of facts.
4. *b* This activity does not demand possession of a prerequisite skill.
5. *b* It is better to have activities involving concrete illustrations for connecting meaning to vocabulary than to read unfamiliar terms.
6. *a* This activity will be immediately successful. Activity *b* requires sustained attention.
7. *a* A kitchen has more environmental relevance than a music store. Creativity training activities should emphasize divergent thinking rather than learning of information.
8. *a* Typically a shy child feels more secure as a member of a group than being featured alone.

THE LEARNER FINDS THE ACTIVITY SATISFYING

Inasmuch as learning takes place when the activity is perceived by the learner as rewarding or satisfying, we must know what the learner has come to value. There are general categories of values which can be appealed to because they are motivating; however, individuals differ in their responses to specific instances within the categories. What one person perceives as humorous another sees as stupid. Hence, in planning learning experiences one must try to find out what has specific appeal, rather than using activities that are generally appealing.

The following motivating categories will help one think of specific ways to make activities more satisfying:

1. *Manipulation* Activities that permit manipulation are enjoyed. Museum exhibits, for instance, become more popular when visitors can make things go, push buttons, construct something, or touch or handle objects.
2. *Incongruity* The exposure to novel and puzzling situations, to events that are inconsistent and incompatible, can be very motivating. Surprising a child with an incongruity—odd sounds, animals dressed as persons—is an excellent way to generate humor. Some incongruous stimuli may be viewed negatively (for example, a situation demanding behavior that conflicts with one's ethics); but when the student "can't believe his eyes" the presentation is likely to get attention, and the resolution of the contradiction through thought and problem-solving can be very rewarding. Significant learning also occurs when the activity allows one to recognize a gap between where he is and where he wants to be.
3. *Interaction with "significant other"* If the activity can involve the learners with the people who are important in their lives—mother, father, grandparent, friend, even teacher—it will be perceived as more satisfying.
4. *Confluence* Activities that combine thinking, feeling, and moving illustrate confluence. For example, a female teacher was interested in having pupils acquire knowledge of the "final *e*" in words. By having pupils represent letters and form themselves as words—some as final *e*'s—she was able to ask, "How does it feel to be the silent *e*?" Her activity was *confluent*—the conceptual, motor, and emotional responses were joined.

28 – THE DESIGN AND SELECTION OF LEARNING ACTIVITIES

Exercise 9 *Identifying motivating categories*

For each activity, indicate which of the following motivating categories is involved:

a. confluence   b. incongruity
c. manipulation   d. significant other

_____ 1. Kindergartners confront intriguing questions, such as How do fish hear?

_____ 2. Dramatic experiments are presented, such as plants shooting seeds.

_____ 3. Students use tape recorders to "write" thoughts.

_____ 4. Students are asked to study in an unexpected place, such as a busy supermarket.

_____ 5. Students are asked to demonstrate new learning to a stranger.

_____ 6. Children learn about the solar system by playing roles of planets and indicating how the different planets feel.

_____ 7. Pupils make something to share with their parents.

_____ 8. Learners pin and label insects using entomologists' procedures.

Answers

1. *b* Incongruity may be a puzzling question.
2. *b* Incongruity may be a dramatic movement.
3. *c* One must manipulate the recorder.
4. *b* Incongruity can be the unusual.
5. *b* The activity is novel (incongruous) to learners. One might pick confluence, however, since there might be emotional involvement.

6. *a* Emphasis is on emotions and feelings.
7. *d* Parents are usually significant others.
8. *c* Psychomotor movement is involved.

Not all individuals will be satisfied by the same activity. The value orientations of different ethnic and cultural groups are currently regarded as important both in explaining individual preferences and in suggesting how to make activities more satisfying. The factors to consider in matching activities with cultural orientation include the following:

1. *Competitive versus cooperative* Learners who prefer to work together on learning tasks should not be required to compete against each other if satisfaction is sought.
2. *Field sensitive versus field insensitive practices* Field sensitive practices are those which foster group or team identity. Field sensitive learners do best in activities where there is much human content (for example, in treatment of personalities rather than abstractions) and much fantasy, humor, and cooperation. Field insensitive learners learn better when the activity features impersonal material.
3. *Socially oriented versus task oriented* The socially oriented person is sensitive to social stimuli and to potential evaluation by others. The task oriented person is primarily interested in the task itself, is achievement oriented, and is less concerned about what others will say about his or her performance. Some learners may be high on both dimensions, and other factors such as *self-assurance* may interact with the dimensions. Social activities — those emphasizing *fun* — are better for socially oriented learners than activities that are structured to focus on proficiency of their learning or on testing their ability.

30 — THE DESIGN AND SELECTION OF LEARNING ACTIVITIES

Exercise 10 *Identifying activities best for learners with particular characteristics*

Look at each description of a learner and then indicate the activity that would be best for that learner.

_____ 1. Field sensitive
   a. Ask the child to provide a personal experience: "Tell when you felt like the characters in this story."
   b. Ask the child to label the emotional state depicted by the character in the story.

_____ 2. Values cooperation
   a. Let those who play their instruments best have the front seats.
   b. No one gets an *A* unless the band is judged best in the competition.

_____ 3. Values competition
   a. Each child does his own work to be compared with the work of others.
   b. Each child works on part of the project, which is judged on its overall merit.

_____ 4. Field insensitive
   a. The learner is encouraged to prepare something for his family.
   b. The learner is encouraged to keep a chart showing his academic progress.

_____ 5. Socially oriented
   a. Ask the pupil to read stories that are "true to life" — stories of wonder and sentiment.
   b. Ask the pupil to read stories to see if they will be fun for the other pupils.

INDIVIDUALIZATION—31

_____ 6. Anxious
   a. The activity demands mastery to a specified criterion.
   b. The activity allows the learner to set his or her own criteria of success.

_____ 7. Self-assured
   a. The activity presents a model or demonstration by a significant other who is to be copied.
   b. The activity involves solving a task without modeling by a significant other.

_____ 8. Verbal
   a. The activity calls for judging evidence used in a debate.
   b. The activity calls for producing synonyms for terms.

Answers

1. *a* The activity requires personal identification rather than intellectual abstraction.
2. *b* The participants must contribute to a group effort.
3. *a* Individualism and rivalry are present.
4. *b* Activity *a* involves the family, something of high priority for the field sensitive person; in *b*, the student's own academic achievement is valued.
5. *b* In this activity, the pupil focuses on concern for others and considers them in a happy setting rather than a work situation.
6. *b* An activity is less threatening when one can set a realistic goal and feel comfortable about it. If one has no way of determining expectations, a demand to set them may be threatening.
7. *b* A self-assured learner can probably perform well in either situation, however.

8. *b* Ability to reason is not the same as verbal ability. Incidentally, Gerald Lesser of Harvard has found that members of ethnic groups differ in their ability to perform on different intellectual tasks.[3]

3. Gerald S. Lesser et al., *Mental Abilities of Children from Different Social Class and Cultural Groups* (Chicago: University of Chicago Press for the Society for Research in Child Development, 1965).

Efficiency — A Fourth Criterion for Judging Learning Activities

Efficiency means consideration of costs in energy, time, materials, and the like. We will look at three common approaches to efficiency in learning activities.

THE PRINCIPLE OF ECONOMY

This principle states that it is wise to select learning opportunities that will contribute to several objectives rather than to just one. Accordingly, when given a choice of a textbook for learning to read that features instruction in comprehension, word recognition, and literary values or one that treats only ways to recognize words, choose the former. Obviously, however, this will be true only when the latter book is also no more effective in helping pupils achieve the single objective.

Interesting illustrations of the use of the principle of economy are found in instructional materials both in communist countries and in our own land. Communists have long advanced particular attitudes toward the United States while presenting academic subject matter. Communist textbooks treating mathematical word

34 — THE DESIGN AND SELECTION OF LEARNING ACTIVITIES

problems, for example, often point to racial discrimination in the United States by asking pupils to determine the ratios of black to white unemployment, income, schooling, etc. Feminists and others in the United States have been quite successful recently in pointing out ways in which prejudicial attitudes have been fostered toward women and minority groups through the pictures, characterizations, and language used in textbooks; and differentiation of activities in physical education, reading, social studies, and other fields.

Exercise 11 *Recognizing multiple objectives from a single activity*

For each activity, indicate the objective(s) to which the activity could contribute.

_____ 1. A field trip to the desert
   a. to analyze the relationship between plants and their environment
   b. to contrast desert animals with familiar animals
   c. to analyze ways man is altering the environment

_____ 2. Step-by-step multiple-choice programmed instruction teaching the metric system
   a. to convert English measurements to the metric system
   b. to type letters without looking at the keyboard
   c. to interpret metaphors

_____ 3. An assignment to contrast audio and visual production techniques of a television program by listening to TV commercials without the picture and watching them without sound
   a. to state how TV communicates
   b. to be more aware of one's senses
   c. to describe nonverbal learning

_____ 4. A new mathematics program rooted in the physical, economic, and social world and involving a variety of devices
   a. to apply mathematics to the everyday world
   b. to like and not be afraid of mathematics
   c. to view mathematics as an abstract field isolated from other bodies of knowledge

_____ 5. Construction of a mini-park (including raising funds, planting grass and trees, constructing benches, etc.)
   a. to develop ways in which citizens can support and use premises of freedom
   b. to acquire skills of persuasion
   c. to be concerned about the needs of others

_____ 6. A satellite-relayed drug program providing facts about drugs
   a. to acquire inquiry skills
   b. to analyze unstated assumptions
   c. to predict probable action knowing individual biases

Answers

1. *a, b, c*   The activity could contribute to all of the outcomes.
2. *a*   There are simpler and more direct ways to achieve the other outcomes.
3. *a, b, c*   The activity could contribute to all outcomes.
4. *a, b*   Outcome *c* is a contradiction.
5. *a, b, c*   The activity could contribute to all of these outcomes and more.
6.   As it stands, the activity is unlikely to contribute to anything more than recall of information. However, activities that would contribute to each of the desired outcomes could be designed around the program.

36 — THE DESIGN AND SELECTION OF LEARNING ACTIVITIES

THE PRINCIPLE OF VARIATION

This principle states that we should use different learning activities to achieve a single objective. The principle rests on three arguments. One is the argument for repetition and related variables. Typical findings from experiments are that several activities are better than one and that more examples, up to ten, are better than few examples, especially in more difficult learning tasks. Second, there is the belief that the continuous use of a single type of learning opportunity — no matter how effective it is in itself — causes learners to lose interest. Third, diagnosis of individual learners' best and preferred approach to learning is costly. Hence, an alternative strategy is to attempt to maximize individualization through a large range of activities, in the hope that at least some of the activities will match the individual's predispositions and strengths.

Exercise 12 *Generating several activities for a single objective*

State below an objective or learning task familiar to you.

Now list three activities which you think would be effective and enjoyable ways to achieve the objective.

Answers

Your answers should have two qualities: (1) the activities should bear an apparent relationship to the objective; and (2) they should use various approaches (discussion, laboratory experiments, audio-visual equipment, case studies, role playing) or involve other variables such as different sensory channels (visual, auditory, tactile).

THE PRINCIPLE OF SIMPLICITY

On one hand, simplicity means trying to make it easier for the learner to recognize patterns that might not be seen in a more complex environment. This occurs when many instances of a natural or social phenomenon can be artificially grouped or manipulated. One might, for example, use ten-minute films showing events that take years to evolve, so that the learner can more readily see abstractions and relationships that would not be obvious in the present and everyday world. On the other hand, the principle of simplicity means that one should choose a simple activity over an elaborate activity when both are focused on the same objective. By way of example, if one is only interested in having pupils recognize the effect of diet on weight, a structured lesson in the classroom will do as well as activities in naturalistic settings.

Advocating a simple activity over a complex one may appear to conflict with the previous recommendation calling for variation, for multiple ways to reach a simple objective. Frankly, it is more a matter of *when* a simple activity will suffice and when varied activities are required. There is a term, *lean programming*, which means, Try to teach with the minimal experience, adding additional activities when it appears necessary. Students need not participate in all variations if they master the task from a single, simple activity.

Another example of simplicity relates to an instrumental value, the principle of appropriate practice. We know that this principle calls for activities by which pupils can practice the behavior stated in the objective. However, it does not mean that all activities must call for behavior identical to that in the objective. Often, it is economical to provide for a form of appropriate practice in which the behavior is *analogous* to that in the objective. Analogous practice takes place when the intellectual operations required by the objective and the learning activity are the same, but overt behavior of the two is different. An objective may say that students will identify propaganda techniques in live speeches by candidates for office, but it may be more efficient to give analogous practice toward this goal by having students identify propaganda techniques used in the editorial pages of newspapers.

Exercise 13 *Recognizing instances of economical practices*

Read each objective and then indicate which activity would call for the same mental operation required by the objective and at less cost.

_____ 1. To differentiate general and specific statements
   a. The pupil will be asked to write examples of general and specific statements.
   b. The pupil will be asked to label lists of statements as general or specific.

_____ 2. To orally recite a poem
   a. The pupil will write the poem without prompts.
   b. The pupil will write an evaluation of the poem.

_____ 3. To identify the question-asking techniques of peers in a teacher-training program
   a. The participant practices identifying questioning techniques as fellow participants instruct.
   b. The participant identifies questioning techniques by viewing film(s) showing teachers instructing.

_____ 4. To interpret emotional states signaled by "body language" (clenched fists, shaking knees, etc.)
   a. The student reads descriptions of persons displaying various physical movements and expressions; he or she then writes the emotional state signified by each description.
   b. The student observes persons in naturalistic settings who might exhibit various movements and expressions; he or she then writes the emotional state signified by each description.

_____ 5. To decode new words
   a. The child hears each word pronounced on a recording as he or she pushes new word cards.
   b. The child applies previously learned elements, such as consonants and vowel-consonant patterns, to read a new word.

_____ 6. To identify different cell structures
   a. The student uses a microscope to draw and label given cell structures.
   b. The student is given drawings of cell structures and asked to label them.

Answers

1. *b*   The objective calls for distinguishing statements, not producing them.

2. *a*   Activity *a* is an example of analogous practice. When large numbers of students are involved, making it difficult to observe oral performance for each person, analogous practice such as in this example may be useful. It does not, of course, take the place of identical practice. Incidentally, practice in production improves judgment more than does practice in judgment.[4] This is one exception to the principle of appropriate practice.

3. *b*   This is appropriate practice. Showing a film may be more economical than trying to arrange for peers to instruct.

4. *a*   This activity is appropriate practice and is more economical than *b*.

5. *b*   Activity *b* demands mental operation of decoding. Activity *a* might be helpful in learning to decode but is not appropriate practice.

6. *b*   This is appropriate practice.

---

4. Donald Johnson, "Cognitive Structures and Intellectual Processes," in *Intellectual Development*, eds. A. Harry Passow and Robert R. Leeper, (Washington, D.C.: Association for Supervision and Curriculum Development, 1964), pp. 27–39.

Summary

As stated in the introduction, learning activities should be reviewed regularly in order to improve on their development and selection. The following checklist will help you analyze activities. The list can facilitate the gathering of information needed for critical assessment and guide the planner in developing activities. It is assumed that participants will judge learning experiences in terms of their own situations.

How does each activity meet the following criteria?	Excellently	Adequately	Fairly	Poorly
1. *Intrinsic qualities*				
a. respects human dignity	——	——	——	——
b. meets aesthetic standards	——	——	——	——
c. other	——	——	——	——
2. *Instrumental values*				
a. evidences task analysis	——	——	——	——
b. provides appropriate practice	——	——	——	——

continued

42 – THE DESIGN AND SELECTION OF LEARNING ACTIVITIES

How does each activity meet the following criteria?	Excel- lently	Ade- quately	Fairly	Poorly
c. draws attention to relevant cues (there are organizers, objectives, prompts, contiguous items, provision for feedback, and confirmation)	_____	_____	_____	_____

3. *Individualization*

   a. allows for learner's experiential background (provides for prerequisites as needed) _____ _____ _____ _____

   b. attempts to make activity satisfying (there is opportunity for manipulation, incongruity, interaction with "significant others," and confluence) _____ _____ _____ _____

   c. allows for different value orientations (cooperative versus competitive, field sensitive versus field insensitive, social versus task orientation) _____ _____ _____ _____

4. *Efficiency*

   a. contributes to more than one objective _____ _____ _____ _____

   b. offers different ways to achieve an objective _____ _____ _____ _____

   c. avoids distracting and irrelevant features (simplifies the learning task) _____ _____ _____ _____

Module 2

DERIVING OBJECTIVES

Chief among the competencies of a curriculum worker is the ability to derive objectives—intended outcomes for programs, courses, learning activities, and the like. Objectives are answers to the question, What do we want our learner to be able to do, know, or feel as a result of the education or training we will provide?

Some say immediately that the question is one of values; that its answer depends on one's definition of a good life, a good person. Others realize that there is a place for empirical studies in determining what outcomes *should* be sought. The latter think that decisions about objectives are better if they take into account findings from the systematic study of current and likely future conditions of life, existing states of knowledge, and the learner's own predispositions and needs.

Deriving objectives is not the same as accepting objectives. Generating highly promising objectives is but a first important step. Choosing the objective that will guide educational planning is a second step. However, the quality of objectives finally accepted will be better if decision-makers can review a range of suggested objectives, all of which are generated through a thoughtful and systematic procedure. The curriculum worker is acting irresponsibly if he or she has no worthy options for the decision-maker.

OBJECTIVES OF THIS MODULE

This module was written to help you achieve the following competencies for generating objectives that merit consideration:

1. The user will be able to name three fruitful sources of data from which to derive objectives.
2. Given lists of questions, the user will be able to identify (a) the questions that are most appropriate for eliciting the kind of

information needed in generating objectives; and (b) the source of information to which those questions should be addressed.
3. Given various kinds of subject matter (descriptions, prescriptions, generalizations, theory), the user will be able to formulate objectives that are consistent with the content of the subject matter.
4. Given facts about learners, the user will be able to use the facts in deciding what to teach.
5. Given data relative to present societal conditions and to the foreseeable future, the user will be able to infer what these data mean for instruction and to formulate an objective that agrees with both data and inference.
6. Given descriptions of decision-making regarding objectives, the user will be able to identify the level (institutional, personal, instructional, societal) at which the decision is being made.

Levels of Decision-Making Regarding Outcomes

A great deal of confusion about the formulation of objectives can be overcome if two ideas are accepted. First, the objectives now held are not necessarily the best. Curriculum construction and planning require continual consideration of desired outcomes and a continual search for new objectives—objectives that may never have been stated before anywhere. Unless one believes that more appropriate ends may be sought, one can never successfully formulate curricular outcomes. Second, the question of *what* to teach—that is, objectives—occurs at four different levels of the educational system:

1. *Societal* Decisions about outcomes are made by legislators of local, state, and federal governments.
2. *Institutional* Decisions about the objectives for a particular school are made by a faculty under the leadership of the principal.
3. *Instructional* A teacher or team of teachers makes decisions about the objectives best for a specific learner or group of learners.
4. *Personal* The learner has much to say about what he or she is to acquire and to become.

48 — DERIVING OBJECTIVES

Decisions made at the more general levels usually influence decisions at the more specific levels. In tight, rational curriculum models, the instructional objectives of the classroom, for example, contribute directly to educational objectives sought by the institution, and the institution's objectives to educational goals set at the societal level. Looser models reflect recognition of opportunities or demands at the more specific levels for objectives unperceived at the more general levels. This is not to say that objectives made at the instructional level, which supplement those of the institution or society level, need oppose objectives found in the organizational hierarchy.

Exercise 1 *Recognizing levels at which objectives are set*

Read the account of objective setting and then indicate the level of decision-making involved.

a. institutional   b. personal   c. instructional   d. societal

_____   1. The teacher realizes that a particular pupil has an unrealistic assessment of his academic ability; hence, the objective is that the pupil will accurately assess his ability.

_____   2. The state assembly responds to concern by a special pressure group about "socialistic tendencies" by setting this objective: that pupils recognize the characteristics and strengths of a free enterprise system.

_____   3. During a unit on poetry, a pupil initiates a request to learn the characteristics of Gaelic poetry.

_____   4. Required by the federal government to do a "needs assessment," the school staff finds that pupils fear tests, so they set an objective calling for pupils to view tests as *helpful.*

5. HEW (a government agency) wants evidence that there is pupil improvement in reading before granting funds to the school staff for continuing a new project.

Answers

1. *c* (*instructional*) A teacher makes the decision.
2. *d* (*societal*) The decision is made by legislation.
3. *b* (*personal*) The learner makes his or her own decision about a desired end.
4. *a* (*institutional*) This is a total staff decision.
5. *d* (*societal*) An arm of the legislature is setting the desired outcome.

Deriving Objectives from Studies of the Learners

PRIMARY AND SECONDARY SOURCES

In studying the learner, the curriculum worker can use two kinds of data sources: primary and secondary. When the curriculum worker goes to learners themselves, he is going to a primary source. Secondary sources are published studies that tell about particular populations of learners. For instance, developmental psychologists tell us about the children who are about to be adolescents — their changing social attitudes, physical growth, intellectual capacities, and the like; sociologists write about the aspirations, self-perceptions, status, and concerns of learners from different socioeconomic and cultural groups.

Exercise 2 *Recognizing the source of data*

Look at the data and indicate whether it is most likely to have been a primary (P) or secondary (S) source for the curriculum worker.

_____ 1. You have asked your pupils to state the family activities that interest them the most.

52—DERIVING OBJECTIVES

_____ 2. One reads that more girls than boys stop their formal education at the close of high school.

_____ 3. A scholar reports two forms of youth counterculture: "cultural"—those who create their own community—and "political"—those who promote a revolutionary program for society.

_____ 4. A common characteristic of young people in the United States is that they are friendly to change; they feel they have no stake in maintaining the status quo.

_____ 5. Nationally, the peak in variety and amount of reading done by boys and girls is at twelve or thirteen years.

_____ 6. Interviews revealed that many ten-year-olds in the school do the shopping and cooking for the family.

_____ 7. Parents in the community report that pupils have certain health practices that are questionable.

Answers

1. P Generalization may be limited to the particular pupils.
2. S Information is obtained from reading—not directly from persons.
3. S Although the data were primary for the scholar, to the curriculum worker the source is secondary.
4. S The wide generalization suggests that it was not directly derived from learners by a curriculum worker.
5. S This fact would have been gathered by someone other than a curriculum worker, although the curriculum worker might use such information in planning.
6. P The data could be easily gathered locally.

DERIVING OBJECTIVES FROM STUDIES OF THE LEARNERS—53

7. *P* The data are primary in the sense that they were likely to have been collected at first hand, locally, rather than gained from some published work that generalizes.

STRATEGIES FOR COLLECTING DATA

A simple approach to data collection is to pick up whatever data one can find about learners. You may see a new book treating problems of youth, or note how few friends a particular learner has. However, such an approach lacks comprehensiveness, and the objectives drawn from the data are not balanced in emphasis. A better approach is to seek data in several categories—physical, intellectual, social, emotional—or to seek the status of particular learners with respect to their strengths and weaknesses in health, recreation, citizenship, vocation, social values (character), academic efforts.

Methods for collecting data from primary sources include observing learners in given situations, using perhaps a checklist; examining the work of learners in order to make inferences about ability, feelings, and attitudes; asking for self-reports through interviews, questionnaires, and interest inventories. Records such as those in the library and the nurse's or counselor's offices are a source of data.

FORMULATING OBJECTIVES FROM DATA COLLECTED

Data are facts from which we can make inferences. Consider, for example, the fact that in late childhood one must begin to build ties with peers, rather than depending only on adults. The curriculum-maker might infer from this fact that the child should acquire social skills valued by peers. Consequently, he or she might derive several objectives involving such abilities as expressing affection, organizing games, considering feelings and privileges of others, and applying principles of fairness.

Exercise 3 *Recognizing objectives derived from facts about the learner*

Consider the six facts that follow, then indicate which objective, *a* or *b*, would be appropriate for the learners to whom each fact applies.

_____ 1. In late childhood, a child begins to understand causal relationships.
   a. to acquire the information that will make tensions of sexual maturity less severe
   b. to describe such physical phenomena as lightning

_____ 2. To become an adult, one must see parents as complex persons, to be emulated in some ways and not in others.
   a. to recognize and weigh values in alternate ways of behaving
   b. to want to please parents in return for love, recognition, and approval

_____ 3. Many college students place sensory experiences ahead of conceptual knowledge.
   a. to acquire validation procedures for moral, aesthetic, and theological knowledge
   b. to devalue detachment, objectivity, and science as methods to truth

_____ 4. Interest and curiosity about sex begins in childhood.
   a. to acquire knowledge of human reproduction
   b. to participate competently in mixed sex sports such as tennis

_____ 5. The preadolescent has better use of small muscles over large periods of time than the young child.
   a. to produce aesthetically pleasing products involving writing, woodwork, sewing, and weaving
   b. to assess realistically one's own interests

_____ 6. The young child sees the world as a "moral realist" (there is no relativity; things are either right or wrong).
   a. to evaluate health beliefs critically
   b. to realize that rules are made by people

Answers

1. *b* Causal relationships are called for in *b*, not in *a*.
2. *a* This objective is consistent with the demand for evaluation.
3. *a* Objective *a* extends an existing situation in a constructive way; objective *b* is limiting and, therefore, not constructive.
4. *a* This end is directly responsive to the stated condition; objective *b* is tangential to the condition.
5. *a* This objective permits the learner to act in accordance with stated strengths.
6. *b* This recognition is a natural stage in the young child's moral growth—"something to work toward."

56 — DERIVING OBJECTIVES

Exercise 4 *Deriving objectives from data about learners*

Read the following paragraph, noting the generalizations it makes. Then select one of the facts and write an objective that you think should follow.

Between nine and twelve years of age, the learner begins to develop a realistic concept of the world. In approach to the physical world, he or she seems to value objective investigation. No longer depending only on adults for answers to "why" questions, the learner will now observe and experiment. His or her achievement of this scientific outlook will determine how he or she will resolve problems of the physical world in the future.

Answers

You might have written an objective that would be helpful to the learner in making observations and experiments. Knowledge of fruitful hypotheses, methods of investigation, provocative problems would make appropriate objectives. Of course, you might have attended to facts about the learner's sense of realism and thereby inferred many other kinds of objectives.

One way to judge the adequacy of your answer is to ask whether it takes into account one of the stated facts and desirable learner growth related to that fact. Desirable growth means either that a gap or deficiency has been closed or that a positive value has been extended.

The Community as a Source of Objectives

There are two principal reasons why studies of particular communities are necessary for vital educational objectives. One reason is that the data from such studies indicate what must be learned if learners are to fit in and contribute to life in that community. The other is that the data reveal local cultural deficiencies that might be alleviated through new objectives and programs.

It ought to be clear that although there can be general information about the conditions of the worldwide community, each nation, state, city, hamlet, or neighborhood requires additional separate study. Although some universal values (such as parents' desire for the survival and physical well-being of their child) are likely to endure everywhere for all times, the best route to these values will be different for each person, society, and period of history. Learning to swim, for example, may be essential to the survival of children in a riverboat community; learning to navigate in traffic may be indispensable in an urban center.

Much of what is learned in school should contribute to desirable actions in the community. But for this transfer to occur, the curriculum planners must know what actions are most needed on "the outside," now and in the future.

DERIVING OBJECTIVES FROM GENERALIZATIONS OFFERED BY STUDENTS OF SOCIETY

The curriculum worker does not always need to make firsthand observations of society in order to derive objectives. Plenty of students of society—sociologists, anthropologists, historians, journalists, political scientists—are doing this continually. Sometimes the scholars specify the educational implications of their findings. At other times, the curriculum worker must derive both the implications and the objectives.

Exercise 5 *Identifying objectives consistent with generalizations*

For each of the following generalizations indicate the educational objective that is consistent with it.

_____ 1. A sociologist concludes that most workers need frequent readjustment to new occupations as their working years pass.
   a. to acquire the specific skills of a given trade
   b. to acquire skills generalizable to a number of fields

_____ 2. A political scientist finds that in the United States there are many ways for citizens to influence legislators; but not all citizens have access to these means.
   a. to illustrate how citizens with different means influence legislators
   b. to identify the characteristics of different citizen groups

3. A futurist perceives a world characterized by temporary relationships and rapid change in technology, values, sexual attitudes, and relationships with family, friends, and organizations.
    a. to recognize the superiority of modern thought to all past forms
    b. to compare and contrast a number of different value systems

4. An economist reports on the finite resources of the earth and the inequity among the world's people in sharing these resources.
    a. to accept the notion of qualitative growth—knowledge, spirit, love—as opposed to the notion of expanding growth in creature comfort and consumer goods
    b. to accept the notion that study of the disciplines—history, physics, math, etc.—is for those who are most intellectually capable and motivated

5. An anthropologist says that the present generation gap is unique, because it is worldwide and because the young sense that their elders, unlike elders in previous generations, do not understand the world.
    a. to ask questions the elders never think to ask, but to trust them enough so that elders will be permitted to join with them in seeking the answers
    b. to describe the way an adolescent acquires status in his society and to contrast this procedure with procedures in other societies

Answers

1. *b* General skills will allow one to adapt to the changed conditions.

60 – DERIVING OBJECTIVES

2. *a* An objective need not resolve the situation but help one understand it.
3. *b* Rapid change requires attention to value conflicts.
4. *a* This objective deals directly with the stated problem.
5. *a* The alternative answer does not deal with the issue of the generation gap.

COLLECTING FIRSTHAND DATA ABOUT THE COMMUNITY

Procedures for collecting data include:

1. looking at successful people and asking what it is that they are able to do and know in situations you deem important
2. identifying critical problems in the community — problems in such areas as health, vocations, recreation, ethics, politics, ecology, social relations
3. surveying the dominant values and cultural perspectives of those in the community, taking care to include samples of different social economic groups
4. making two kinds of predictions about foreseeable future life in the community: (a) what it will be like if present trends continue; and (b) what it *should* be like to satisfy the requirements of an ideal community
5. introspecting — thinking about your own experiences in some aspects of life in the community, including the problems you encounter and the needs you have

Exercise 6 *Deriving objectives from data about the community*

Read the following facts collected by the staff of a local school and derive an educational objective from each fact (that is, tell what learners should be able to do or know in light of the fact presented).

1. Health records reveal that venereal disease is at epidemic level. An appropriate objective is:

2. Newspaper accounts reporting actions before local governing bodies show that the community must make crucial decisions about environment and developmental growth. An objective is:

3. In a local industry that is likely to offer employment to graduates, most highly rated employees display these characteristics: initiative in work situations, persistency in task, and willingness to receive and act on criticism. An appropriate objective is:

4. Your community will soon be using the metric system for most of its computation. An appropriate objective is:

62 – DERIVING OBJECTIVES

Answers

1. Your objectives might have included: to recognize causes of venereal diseases (respond with information), to value the human body (respond with attitudes), to respect the dignity of others (respond with attitudes). Your answer should be one that will help learners to deal with the problem.
2. Again, your answer should help learners deal with the situation by interpreting the issues, weighing the probable consequences of one policy against those of another, or weighing their own values in the matter. It should be clear that your objective is an educational response. As an educator, you are not necessarily responsible for resolving the social problems, particularly when there are critical factors that you cannot control.
3. Any objective that would foster the qualities mentioned would be acceptable. One example is: the learner will persist in completing assignments. However, this example gives rise to the optional view that the school should not prepare the learners for what *is*, but help the learner critique what is. Hence, an objective that calls for evaluation of the situation would also be appropriate. Your objective might be to evaluate employment practices, or to assess the employment opportunities in the community and elsewhere.
4. An objective that would meet the situation might be: to compute in the metric system.

Deriving Objectives from Subject Specialists

There are many separate subjects that can be studied; one scholar lists nearly a thousand. In each field—in math, history, physics, linguistics—there are persons devoted to studying the classes of phenomena or problems associated with the subject matter, creating and using concepts and tools for investigating the problems, and testing the validity of their findings.

Sometimes curriculum planners are interested in having students prepare to take a worker's place in one of the subjects as a creator of knowledge—a specialist. At other times, the curriculum planner is only interested in "raiding" the subject matter, taking out the findings, conclusions, methods, or concepts from a subject that might be valuable to all learners, not just future specialists.

Exercise 7   *Recognizing objectives derived from subject matter*

Each of the following items contains either a statement *about* a particular subject (such as its function) or a statement of content (concepts or method *in* the subject). Indicate which objective is derived from each statement.

64 — DERIVING OBJECTIVES

_____ 1. *Anthropology* One of the central ideas of this subject is the concept of *culture*. This term refers to the symbolic devices, institutions, and things contrived by man. They are the results of man's efforts to "improve" nature.
   a. to identify the universal needs that are met by different structures and organizations
   b. to characterize various California shallow water fish (rare, endangered, etc.)

_____ 2. *Humanistic psychology* A new school of psychology holds that expression of feelings and emotional honesty are necessary for emotional health; further, that meaning and human awareness are expanded when one allows all the senses to receive.
   a. to acquire knowledge of morals and manners, particularly that knowledge transmitted by words, demonstrated acts, and nonverbal symbols in science, art, religion, and other fields
   b. to acquire such techniques for self-discovery as aikido, Gestalt, Rolfing, autogenic training, bioenergetics, zen meditation, sensual massage, and biofeedback

_____ 3. *Linguistics* The American English sentence should be read not as a sequence of words but as a unitary and meaning-bearing sequence of structures signaled by such factors as intonation, sentence order, and "empty" words that mark different kinds of meaning.
   a. to identify the words in sentences that mark questions and clauses; in reading orally, to give heavy stress to only one word in a sentence and to identify the word order associated with a request or command
   b. to identify high frequency "sight" words; to acquire phonic generalizations such as the effect of the final *e* or vowel sound of a word; and in reading silently to avoid vocalization and movement of the lips

_____ 4. *Mathematics* Function is one of the most significant concepts in mathematics. It helps illuminate the idea that events do not always occur haphazardly. To learn functions is to learn relations among things, the nature of rational meaning.
   a. to realize that demonstrated propositions in mathematics are certain and indisputable for all time
   b. to recognize simple related magnitudes in various forms; to be able to find the output when given the input in simple problems

_____ 5. *Art* The principle of individualism is a major contribution of art. Unlike scientists' interest in similarities and conformities, the artist attends to the unique, the different, the unrepeatable.
   a. to classify music as "jazz" and "classical"; to analyze architecture as "Gothic" and "Georgian"
   b. to make an original drawing that displays the qualities of "balanced contrast" and "unity"; to create a short story that has both a "climax" and "denouement"

Answers

1. *a* This objective deals with anthropological concepts.
2. *b* Objective *b* emphasizes personal over objective knowledge as does humanistic psychology.
3. *a* This answer is consistent with linguistic notion of meaning.
4. *b* Only this answer deals with mathematical functions.
5. *b* Objective *b* focuses on originality rather than on type.

QUESTIONS ONE MAY ASK WHEN LOOKING AT GENERALIZATIONS FROM SUBJECT SPECIALISTS

All curriculum-makers do not have the opportunity to go in person to those who are winning knowledge in a given field. We have to depend on the writings of the specialist or of someone who has studied the specialist's work. Committees that prepare yearbooks and other publications for professional organizations (for example, the National Council of Teachers of English, the School Mathematics Study Group, or the Commission on Mental Illness and Health) often report both important developments in a field and the implications of these developments for what should be taught. Individual authors writing in professional journals also suggest educational objectives from their review of scholars' basic works. Textbook writers, too, attempt to reflect summaries of important generalizations from the growing edge of knowledge.

There are questions each consumer of scholarship should ask whether he or she is seeking fruitful generalizations from the specialist directly or from interpreters.

1. What generalizations can you suggest that are basic to understanding the subject?
2. Do you have generalizations that will facilitate later learning in the school?
3. What generalizations will help one use his or her experiences outside the school in a more educative manner?
4. What generalizations do you have that will increase the learner's ability to generate new questions, or to conceptualize alternatives and their consequences?

Exercise 8 *Deriving Objectives from Subject Matter*

Select one of the generalizations below and then formulate an educational objective that might follow.

_____ 1. Algorisms are important in almost every branch of mathematics. In developing an algorism, we must construct a detailed step-by-step plan. Flow charting offers insight into the nature of algorisms.

_____ 2. One essential of historical method is to collect records of the past; a second essential is to choose a point of view, value system, or interpretive scheme for deciding what records to collect and analyze.

_____ 3. The biological concept of evolution has import for the attitudes we hold. Evolutionists hold that whatever happens now will tend to make a difference in the future; each generation is a link in the evolutionary chain.

Answers

1. You could have stated such objectives as: to interpret flow charts; to express simple mathematical algorisms in flow chart

68 — DERIVING OBJECTIVES

form; to identify algorisms in computer programming; to construct a step-by-step plan for a given operation.
2. You might have stated objectives such as: to interpret events from the point of view of economics, struggles (moral or military), great leaders, psychological motivation, etc.; to identify records available for the study of history.
3. You might have derived objectives such as: to predict the probable consequences of particular existing biological conditions, to illustrate how evolution might occur indirectly through natural selection, to give examples of how things, beliefs, and practices are handed on in cultural evolution.

Exercise 9 *Recognizing sources of data for deriving objectives*

Put an X by useful questions to ask in deriving objectives. Then indicate which data source should be consulted:
a. learner   b. society   c. subject matter

_____ 1. What is the incidence of venereal disease?

_____ 2. What concepts will transfer to future learning in the field?

_____ 3. What subject matter concepts will transfer to daily living?

_____ 4. How many teachers are in the school?

_____ 5. What kinds of work will there be in the future?

_____ 6. What physiological changes are the children experiencing?

_____ 7. What emotional needs of pupils are not being fulfilled?

_____ 8. What textbooks are used in the school?

_____ 9. Should we have nongraded schools?

_____ 10. What principles connect many facts, thereby facilitating memory?

Answers

Useful questions are: 1, 2, 3, 5, 6, 7, and 10. Questions 4, 8, and 9 might be asked after the objectives are formulated and accepted. Answers to the latter questions are only relevant to the attainment of the objectives, not their formulation.

Learner as a source: questions 6 and 7. *Society* as a source: questions 1 (community health) and 5 (vocational future). *Subject matter* as a source: questions 2, 3, 10.

Your successful answers show that you are able to generate educational objectives. The next step is to be able to make defensible choices from many possible objectives. There are always many more objectives than can be achieved; hence the curriculum worker must know how to determine their importance.

Summary

Some people prize the objectives they are already using, believing that these will be relevant to most persons at all times and places. Such persons are unlikely to want to know how to derive objectives. Others, however, do not believe in a final set of objectives. Instead, they believe that they can always improve their ends-in-view in light of new conditions and the status of particular learners. For them, observing both learners and circumstances is a vital step in the setting of purposes. That is not to say that it is a sufficient step. Such people must use their intelligence and judgment to determine the data that should be collected and the significance of what is found.

By responding to the following questions, you will be able to assess your commitment to a systematic generation of objectives and at the same time think through the specific procedures that seem best for your own situations.

_____ 1. For what level of decision-making are you most likely to derive objectives?
   a. societal
   b. institutional

72 — DERIVING OBJECTIVES

      c. instructional
      d. personal

_____ 2. What type(s) of source will you use?
      a. primary
      b. secondary
      c. both primary and secondary

_____ 3. What sources for data will you use?
      a. the learner
      b. society
      c. subject matter specialists
      d. other

_____ 4. If you will use the learner as a source, what kinds of data will you seek?
      a. the learner's dynamic needs, such as the need for affection
      b. the learner's gaps in knowledge, skills, and attitudes
      c. the learner's own interests and purposes

_____ 5. If you will use society as a source, what kinds of data will you seek?
      a. present social conditions
      b. likely future social conditions

_____ 6. If you will use data from specialists, what information will you seek?
      a. scholars' beliefs about what is necessary for success in their respective fields
      b. scholars' beliefs about what in their fields is most relevant for all citizens

_____ 7. Which additional means will you use in deriving objectives?
      a. exemplars or models
      b. discrepancies between ideals and the current status

Module 3

SELECTING AMONG EDUCATIONAL OBJECTIVES – DEFENSIBLE CHOICES

A curriculum worker can usually generate more objectives than he or she can teach in any situation. The attempt to meet a large number of objectives will fail because achievement depends on focus. No one has enough energy, time, and resources to fulfill all possible outcomes. How then can one decide which of many objectives is the most crucial? There are three models that one can use: (1) the needs assessment model, (2) a philosophical model, and (3) a psychological model. Although these models have many features in common, you will want to judge them on the basis of their practicality, comprehensiveness, and logical consistency.

OBJECTIVES OF THIS MODULE

The user of this module should achieve these competencies:

1. Using a cruciality formula, the user will be able to determine the cruciality of proposed objectives.
2. The user will be able to describe the steps of a needs assessment approach to curriculum-making.
3. The user will be able to eliminate objectives on the basis of their inconsistency with views of realist, idealist, and pragmatist philosophies.
4. The user will be able to recognize five major conflicting viewpoints regarding the curriculum and to identify objectives acceptable in accordance with each of these viewpoints.
5. The user will be able to estimate the difficulty of educational objectives using factors for determining feasibility.
6. The user will be able to accept and reject objectives on the basis of Piaget's developmental theory.
7. The user will be able to determine his or her own fundamental beliefs about schooling and learning and to relate these beliefs to curriculum-making.

The Needs Assessment Approach to Selecting Educational Objectives

Needs assessment can occur at all curriculum decision-making levels. Those responsible for a school district may use the technique to determine the district's goal priorities; the staff in a particular school might conduct a needs assessment to determine the objectives that will guide program planning; individual teachers can conduct a needs assessment to determine the most important objectives for given pupils in reading, mathematics, human relations, or other areas. Although procedures may be different when needs are assessed at different levels, all assessments of needs should include four basic activities:

1. listing all the objectives from which the most important are to be selected
2. receiving preferences from various persons (parents, students, peers) regarding the relative value of each objective
3. assessing the degree to which the population of interested learners have achieved the objectives
4. determining the most important objectives in light of both preference and magnitude of discrepancy in learner status

80 — SELECTING AMONG EDUCATIONAL OBJECTIVES

The list of objectives may be generated by curriculum workers (as explained in Module 2) or obtained from commercial and professional sources. Further, parents, pupils, and others who will be directly affected may want to submit their own objectives for consideration. The question of who should participate in reviewing the list is an open one. The old guideline, "those who will be affected by the decision," might be followed as far as possible. Consideration of expert opinion is also valid. How the list is to be reviewed is another question. Usually one thinks of such procedures as (1) sending out lists of objectives and asking individual respondents to rank the objectives' importance, or (2) having groups of persons place cards (each card with a different objective) in five piles, each pile indicating a degree of preference. A fixed percentage of cards must be placed on all piles. However, before such procedures are followed, all participants should participate in a "reflective session" using the *cruciality formula*.

THE REFLECTIVE SESSION AND CRUCIALITY FORMULA

$$\text{Cruciality} = \frac{\begin{pmatrix}\text{probability that} \\ \text{the learner will need} \\ \text{objective (rate: 1-5,} \\ \text{with 5 as highest probability)}\end{pmatrix} \times \begin{pmatrix}\text{probability that} \\ \text{the objective is} \\ \text{attainable} \\ \text{(rate: 1-5)}\end{pmatrix}}{\begin{pmatrix}\text{probability that} \\ \text{the objective would occur} \\ \text{in a nonschool setting} \\ \text{(rate: 1-5)}\end{pmatrix}}$$

The above cruciality formula might be used in the following way. At a faculty meeting, some members present the objectives they believe to be most important for their curriculum for the teaching of reading. In order to decide which of these objectives should have priority, they apply the cruciality formula. The members take one objective and then proceed as follows:

1. Estimate the probability of learner need. In other words, what evidence do you have (a) that learners are interested in the objective, (b) that the objective meets basic needs (social, physiological, integrative) of the learners, and (c) that the objective will be needed both in future learning at school and in the community? After answering these questions, members indicate (by a show of hands) their estimate of probability: 1, 2, 3, 4, or 5. A single average score for the group is placed in the formula as the probability of learner need.
2. Estimate that the objective is teachable. What evidence is there that the objective is achievable? Consider such constraints as time and materials. Does the objective demand a large number of prerequisites not in the learner's repertoire? How much is known about how to teach to the objective? Is a minimal mental or maturation factor required for success in learning the objective? After discussion, a collective mean score indicating the estimated probability is recorded in the formula as shown, and the numbers for teachability and learner need are multiplied.
3. Estimate the probability that the objective will be realized in a nonschool setting. Members must consider whether other educational agencies will focus on the objective. *Sesame Street* and *Electric Company* objectives might be considered, for example, before assigning priority to the school's objectives in the teaching of reading. The staff will, of course, note the fact that such nonschool objectives may not be available to all learners. Those objectives likely to be achieved "just by living in the community" will be given a higher estimate of probability. After discussion, a collective mean score indicating the group's estimate is recorded for nonschool probability, and

82—SELECTING AMONG EDUCATIONAL OBJECTIVES

this number is divided into the product of the teachability and learner need values to indicate the value of the objective.

In this fashion, other objectives are reviewed, and the relative value of each objective is shown by the final scores.

Exercise 1 *Applying the cruciality formula to objectives*

For each of the three objectives listed below, estimate the probabilities (within a range of 1–5) of need, teachability, and occurrence in a nonschool situation. When estimating the probabilities, think of a situation including a learner or learners familiar to you. Then find the cruciality value for the objective by using the following formula.

$$\frac{\text{probability of need (1-5)} \times \text{probability of achievement (1-5)}}{\text{probability that it will be learned out of school (1-5)}}$$

1. Learners will show reduced anxiety toward tests, peers, and adults in the school.

$$\frac{(\quad) \times (\quad)}{(\quad)}$$

2. Learners will resolve moral problems in accordance with ethical principles instead of self-interest.

$$\frac{(\quad) \times (\quad)}{(\quad)}$$

3. Learners will be willing to engage in tasks involving reading or learning to read when asked.

$$\frac{(\quad) \times (\quad)}{(\quad)}$$

Answers

One group that applied the formula obtained the following results:

1. $\dfrac{3 \times 3}{2} = 4.5$

2. $\dfrac{4 \times 1}{4} = 1$

3. $\dfrac{4 \times 4}{2} = 8$

Members of this group believed that although all of the objectives were needed by learners, objective 2 was not likely to be achieved by their learners, who were operating at much lower levels of moral behavior. Further, they believed that other agencies in the community were assuming responsibility for this task.

MEASURING THE GAP BETWEEN LEARNERS' PRESENT STATUS AND THE OBJECTIVE

Objectives that receive high preferences are not necessarily the objectives that should receive the highest priority. In making a needs assessment, one should have a rule stating how much weight one will give to preferences and how much to the gap between ideal and present status. The needs assessment requires measurement of the present status of the learners with respect to the objective. This calls for matching an assessment measure with the objective and collecting data on learner status. Several procedures and techniques are available for this purpose including observations, self-reports, records, and tests (see Module 4 on Evaluation).

84 — SELECTING AMONG EDUCATIONAL OBJECTIVES

Exercise 2 *Determining the priority of objectives on the basis of both discrepancy and preference*

In the table below, four objectives have been ranked according to preference (5 is highest) and magnitude of discrepancy between present and desired learner state (5 indicates the greatest gap). Your task is to rank the objectives according to priority (write 5 opposite the objective of highest priority, 4 opposite the next in priority, etc.).

Objectives	Preference rank	Discrepancy rank	Priority
A	2	3	_____
B	4	2	_____
C	3	5	_____
D	5	4	_____

Answers

Objective D should probably be given the highest priority, especially because it is first in preference and second in size of gap.

Objective C should receive next priority in view of the severe difference between the present and desired states for learners.

In order to determine priorities of the remaining objectives, you should formulate a rule for weighing preferences and deficiencies.

Philosophical Models

Exercise 3 *Recognizing inconsistencies between objectives and philosophies*

The following exercise will give you some idea of how philosophy can be used to decide which objectives are acceptable. Statements associated with three major philosophical positions—idealism, realism, and pragmatism—are given.

Also, four objectives are presented. Your task is to see whether or not each of the objectives would be consistent with the respective positions. Write *yes* or *no* in the space provided indicating whether the objective would be acceptable to those who hold the following philosophies.

1. *Idealist* Ideal qualities of beauty, goodness, and justice are changeless. Learners should have models of ideals to emulate. Teachers should know what is best for learners to learn.
2. *Realist* We must comprehend the structure of the universe; therefore, knowledge and reason must be cultivated and we should pass on the findings of authorities. Learners must know these findings before attempting to improve the world.

3. *Pragmatist* Education is reconstruction of experience. Truth is man-made and consists of workable ideas. Adjustment of the individual to harmonious physical and social relations is important. We should encourage questioning and experimentation.

Objectives	Idealist	Realist	Pragmatist
1. To write convincing arguments for and against abortion	___	___	___
2. To observe without questioning a demonstration proving that light is necessary for photosynthesis	___	___	___
3. To make moral decisions, "being true to oneself" (acting in accordance with personal preference rather than some external standard)	___	___	___
4. To judge paintings from different periods by applying universal criteria	___	___	___

Answers

1. Idealist   No   The principle of respect for life is eternal.
   Realist   Yes This objective aids reasoning.
   Pragmatist Yes Questioning is a value.
2. Idealist   Yes The teacher conveys the truth.
   Realist   Yes Learners must comprehend the universe, not create it.

	Pragmatist	*No*	There is no experimentation on the part of the learner.
3.	Idealist	*No*	Eternal standards should dominate.
	Realist	*No*	Truth is universal, not idiosyncratic.
	Pragmatist	*Yes*	But individuals must consider consequences.
4.	Idealist	*Yes*	The standards of beauty are changeless.
	Realist	*Yes*	Beauty is objective, not subjective.
	Pragmatist	*No*	Values are relative to the situation.

EDUCATIONAL PHILOSOPHIES

Some curriculum workers prefer to have those responsible for a school's program choose one of the following educational philosophies before attempting to accept or reject specific proposed objectives.

1. *Perennialism*   Values do not change; they are perennial. The primary function of education is intellectual development. The truth is everywhere the same; hence education should be the same everywhere. Perennialists believe that the most powerful ideas of human intelligence are found for the most part in the established academic disciplines. A general, liberal education that stresses verbal ability is most practical—more practical than vocational education because it makes persons more versatile, circumspect, and fulfilled. As academic rationalists, perennialists could teach both the concepts and methods of their academic disciplines and the works of art that have withstood the test of time.
2. *Social reconstructionism, relevance*   Emphasis should be on the role of the school within the larger social context; societal needs are more important than individual needs. Social reform

and responsibility to the future of society are primary. Schooling should be an instrument by which society changes itself. Students should learn to deal with social issues and be involved in the community to effect change. The school should help one learn what the facts are in our social conflicts and to perceive the values that are at stake.

3. *Essentialism* Schools are for teaching the essentials—the three R's, oral expression, English, history, government, geography, foreign languages, mathematics, sciences. The curriculum is fairly fixed.

4. *Psychological cognitivism* There are independent cognitive skills that can be taught and that will transfer to a variety of situations. Cognitive processes and problem-solving are what learners should be taught. Hypotheses and strategies such as how to avoid repeating incorrect answers are also important learnings. Processes such as abstracting, analyzing, classifying, equating, inferring, and sequencing are mental skills that the school should teach.

5. *Self-Actualism* Schooling should be a means to personal fulfillment and provide the content and tools for self-discovery. The school should help the individual achieve integration and personal growth. This may mean attention to mental health, because one who is beset with fears and conflicts cannot effectively realize his or her goals. It also means concentrating on having the emotions, intelligence, habit, and body reinforce each other. A multidisciplinary curriculum is needed to fulfill this concern for wholeness. Schooling must be a vital and enriching experience in its own right. The curriculum should not be characterized so much by the objective content of studies as by the atmosphere created by the participants.

Exercise 4 *Using educational philosophies to accept and eliminate proposed objectives*

Read each objective and then indicate which educational philosophy would *exclude* the objective.

_____ 1. To come to terms with the meaning of death
   a. essentialism
   b. self-actualism

_____ 2. To raise questions and set one's own purposes
   a. cognitivism
   b. social reconstructionism

_____ 3. To state the masks humans hide behind, to express what is personal
   a. essentialism
   b. self-actualism

_____ 4. To form friendships across racial lines
   a. social reconstructionism
   b. cognitivism

_____ 5. To suggest new lines of investigation in a subject field based on observations
   a. cognitivism
   b. essentialism

_____ 6. To accept the idea that the pursuit of individual gain does not constitute an obstacle to the progress of the group
   a. self-actualism
   b. social reconstructionism

90 — SELECTING AMONG EDUCATIONAL OBJECTIVES

Answers

1. *a*   A self-actualist would accept this objective as vital.
2. *b*   A strategy for raising questions is a cognitive skill. The setting of one's purpose does not put society first as the reconstructionists do.
3. *a*   An essentialist is not interested in the personal but in the same requirements for all.
4. *b*   The cognitivist is interested in intellectual more than affective and social behavior. The social reconstructionist seeks to develop community and share values.
5. *b*   Unlike the cognitivist who encourages problem solving, the essentialist does not expect the student to discover new truths.
6. *b*   The social reconstructionist believes that the attempt to be more human individually is egotism, a form of dehumanization.

Exercise 5   *Developing your own philosophical assumptions to use in "screening" objectives*

Give your answer to each of the following questions:

1. Is the purpose of a school to change, adapt to, or accept the social order?

2. What can a school do better than any other agency or institution?

3. What objectives should be common to all?

4. Should objectives stress cooperation or competition?

5. Should attitudes be taught? Fundamental skills? Problem-solving strategies?

6. Should objectives deal with all controversial issues, or only those for which there is established knowledge?

7. Should teachers emphasize subject matter or try to create behavior outside of school?

8. Should objectives be based on needs of the local community? Society in general? Expressed needs of the student?

Answers

There are at least three criteria you can apply to your answers. One is *consistency*. If, for example, you conceived of the role of the school as helping pupils accept the social order, then other answers should follow; for example, in question 3, a common objective might be citizenship—to obey the Bill of Rights.

Another criterion is *comprehensiveness*. You might have considered many factors. For instance, you could have seen that in some situations, different answers to the same questions would be acceptable. On question 8, you might have noted that a school could have concurrently (1) an academic program based on knowledge of importance to society as a whole, (2) a "daily living" practicum in which there are objectives reflecting the needs of the local community, and (3) "an elective program" in which the learner can seek his or her own purposes.

A third criterion is *specificity*. If your answers were specific enough they may help you to eliminate objectives. For instance, it is easier to screen objectives with an answer to question 2 that says "to socialize—to learn to work with pupils of different backgrounds," than with a general expression such as "to educate."

Psychological Models for Deciding What to Teach

Whereas philosophical models may help you decide what *should* and *should not* be taught, psychological models contribute to your decision of what to teach showing what *can* be taught and *when*.

FEASIBILITY OF OBJECTIVES

The feasibility of an objective depends on at least three factors. One of these is the *learning task* itself. An easy task may require short-term memory, and involve few items of information to be coordinated; a difficult task may require lengthy retention and processing of many items of information.

A second factor is the *capacity of the learner*. Knowledge of both the learner's maturation and point of view regarding the learning task enables the curriculum specialist to estimate task feasibility.

A third factor is *knowledge of the instructional sequence*, that is, the extent to which the task has been analyzed and provision made for teaching prerequisite concepts and skills not in the learner's repertoire. Briefly, feasibility depends on knowledge of what makes up a task and clear criteria for judging the learner's responses.

The difficulty of teaching to a goal of creativity as opposed to teaching to a goal of typewriting may be due to lack of task specificity, knowledge of prerequisites, and clear criteria for judging correctness of responses.

Exercise 6 *Estimating the difficulty of educational objectives*

Within each set of objectives indicate which of the two tasks given is more difficult, then underline the answer that best explains why that task is more difficult.

_____ 1. Objectives for nine- to eleven-year-old learners
   a. to design carefully controlled experiments
   b. to perform the computations of subtraction, multiplication, and division
      1. The task analysis is incomplete.
      2. The learner lacks motor coordination.
      3. The task is unrewarding.

_____ 2. Objectives for field sensitive adults without knowledge of mechanics
   a. to become mechanically competent (for example, to display the technical skills of an automobile repairman)
   b. to become field insensitive (for example, to inhibit one's natural response to a stimulus and instead exhibit a response that is logically correct)
      1. The learner lacks maturity.
      2. The relevant dimensions of the task are not clear.
      3. There is no criterion for correct responses.

_____ 3. Objectives for eight-year-old learners
   a. to spell correctly words presented in spelling books
   b. to solve new problems that parallel those in their math books
      1. The task requires abstract rather than associative learning.
      2. The task elements have not been analyzed.
      3. The learner lacks maturity.

_____ 4. Objectives for teaching an adolescent whose cultural orientations are different from the dominant culture found in the school
   a. to acquire a different attitude toward oneself (for example, a positive self-concept)
   b. to acquire a different attitude toward the school (for example, a belief that school is a friendly and helpful place)
      1. The learner has a point of view that is not consistent with the task.
      2. The learner lacks the necessary maturity.
      3. The learner cannot coordinate the number of subskills required.

Answers

1. *a, 1*   There are insufficient specifications of all elements involved in designing controlled experiments. Also the task is more difficult because it is abstract, not just associated learning.
2. *b, 2*   We do not know what factors produce field sensitivity and field insensitivity.
3. *b, 1*   Solving new problems is a transfer problem rather than simple paired associative learning.

4. *a, 1*   Self-evaluations are generally stable and difficult to change. Attitudes toward objects and institutions not immediately related to the self are easier to change than attitudes based on early home and religious training.

DESCRIPTIVE AND THEORETICAL MODELS

Popular literature describes what typical learners do at different years of age; a five-year-old, for example, can hop on one foot for ten seconds, climb trees, walk on a chalked straight line, and run on tiptoes. Although such data may provide evidence supporting the feasibility of particular objectives for given learners, they may also be misleading.

Observation of what *is achieved* under the status quo does not always indicate what *is possible.* Children now ride two-wheeled bikes at five, although some years ago we thought they could not ride two-wheelers until they were ten. Ten was the age at which children were then first riding bicycles. It is true, too, that with changes in nutrition, greater immunity to disease, and the like, youngsters are reaching maturity much sooner than before.

There is also a danger in concluding what is possible on the basis of inferences drawn from theories. For example, the brain plasticity theory suggests that the young child has a "cerebral receptivity" to language acquisition, which may be a function of the brain or lack of cortical specialization. Hence it was thought that the individual's capacity to learn a language decreases as the brain becomes more specialized, with speech lateralized in the left cerebral hemisphere. It was therefore suggested that foreign language instruction begin before age ten to take advantage of this critical period in developing good foreign language skill, such as "native-like pronunciation." Recently, however, Olson and Samuels[1] found evidence that contradicts the theory. The results of their well-controlled experiment not only failed to show that younger children were able to produce a *more* native-like accent than older people; but they showed that the trend is in a reverse direction, favoring older students.

Some learning does, however, depend on maturation. No one is going to teach a child to walk at the age of six months, and it is far more economical to teach a child to climb stairs at fifty-three rather than at forty-three weeks.

DEVELOPMENTAL PSYCHOLOGY AND THE PLACEMENT OF OBJECTIVES

Developmentalists like Piaget[2] and Kohlberg[3] have proposed a number of stages through which the learner progresses. Although the rate of progress is not fixed, these theories hold that the sequence among the stages is. Therefore, if the curriculum worker knows what stage the learner is in, she or he might be able to compare proposed objectives with the stage to determine both feasibility and placement.

---

1. Linda Olson and Jay Samuels, "The Relationship Between Age and Accuracy of Foreign Language Pronunciation," *The Journal of Educational Research* 66, no. 6 (February 1973).
2. J. Piaget, *Science of Education and the Psychology of the Child* (New York: Orion, 1970).
3. L. Kohlberg, "Implications of Developmental Psychology for Education," *Educational Psychologist* 10 (1973):2–4.

98 — SELECTING AMONG EDUCATIONAL OBJECTIVES

Exercise 7 *Using Piaget's stages of cognitive growth to accept and eliminate objectives*

Read each statement and the objective that follows. Then indicate whether one should accept (A) or reject (R) the objective on the basis of the match between learner and theory.

_____ 1. *The sensorimotor period (birth to 2 years)* To the learner, objects are transitory, lasting as long as sight, sound, or touch. The learner cannot conceive hierarchically organized plans. A child acquires a "practical intelligence" during this period by which he can keep track of an object's location and make detours.

Objective for a one-year old The learner will be able to follow instructions on how to get to the kitchen, to a toy, or to a pet.

_____ 2. *The preoperational period (ages 2–7)* The child is able to let one thing stand for another. A pebble can represent a piece of candy; the pebble is a *symbol*. Child may also use a *sign*, saying "candy" when pretending to eat the pebble. The child lacks ability to focus attention on the multiple aspects of a situation; he or she will look at either the level of water in a jar or the width of the jar, not both. The child also finds it difficult to take another person's point of view.

Objective for a five-year-old The learner will be able to interpret what the feelings and outlooks of a child from another culture might be in a given situation.

3. *The period of concrete operations (7–12)* The learner can perform cognitive operations such as combining, separating, or adding and subtracting. When coordinating these operations, the learner can consider two aspects of a situation at once and see their systematic relations. Reversability is involved in all instances of concrete operational thinking; for example, the effect of an increase in length of a piece of clay is reversed by a reciprocal decrease in its diameter. The child cannot apply operations to hypothetical situations, only to "concrete," or actual ones. That is, the child can't apply logic to arrive at an answer when the situation given contradicts what he or she knows to be a fact.

    Objective for a ten-year-old The learner will be able to identify valid logical conclusions drawn from statements expressed in various conditional formats. One example would be: If John smokes a lot, then he has cancer; if John does not have cancer, does that mean he does not smoke a lot?

4. *The period of formal operations (12–)* The learner can project beyond his or her actual experience. He or she can systematically generate a set of possibilities or hypotheses, and devise a plan for testing them (for example, the learner can vary one thing at a time while holding everything else constant). The ability to conceive and reason about hypothetical possibilities provides a basis for scientific thinking.

    Objective for an adolescent Given a phenomenon not previously studied involving two different outcomes, the learner will be able to explain the data and propose a way to check out the explanation.

Answers

1. R Learners at this stage cannot respond to verbal instructions without concrete referents.
2. R Learners at this stage cannot take another's point of view.
3. R Learners at this stage cannot engage in formal logic.
4. A Learners at this stage can devise plans for testing hypotheses.

CAVEAT

Competent scholars such as Ennis[4] have criticized Piaget's basis for judging the adequacy of children's thinking. Also, there have been reports of successful curriculum projects which accepted objectives that did not clear Piaget's filter. The planners of *Sesame Street*, for instance, chose as one of their objectives for three- and four-year-olds the following: "Able to take another's point of view, to understand that another person may see and feel differently from the way you do and then be able to imagine yourself in the person's place." Although Piaget estimates this as an advanced skill that would not be acquired before the period of the third stage (age 7), the objective was achieved.

Closing on a philosophical note, I would like to point out that it would be a mistake to regard as final current psychological definitions of what is possible. In spite of our visible limitations and failures as human beings, we still have awesome untapped capabilities. Most of us are operating with only a tiny fraction of our true abilities. Perhaps there will be better ways to unlock man's vast potential and, thereby, permit us to accept more of our proposed objectives.

4. Robert Ennis, "Children's Ability to Handle Piaget's Propositional Logic: A Conceptual Critique," *Review of Educational Research* 45, no. 1 (Winter 1975).

Summary

By taking a position on each of the following statements, an individual or a group can readily identify fundamental views of schooling and learning. These views can then help one to eliminate or accept proposed objectives. Further, if you compare your responses with existing objectives (noting how well the valued items are provided for in the school's present program) you will see the need for previously unrecognized objectives.

	Strongly agree	*Agree*	*Disagree*	*Strongly disagree*
1. The major purpose of school is				
a. to cultivate the rational powers—academic excellence.	_____	_____	_____	_____
b. to develop individual potential in accordance with one's own choices.	_____	_____	_____	_____

continued

	Strongly agree	Agree	Disagree	Strongly disagree
c. to build a community more in keeping with our ideals.	———	———	———	———
d. to show how to learn.	———	———	———	———

2. Social goals of the school are:

	Strongly agree	Agree	Disagree	Strongly disagree
a. furthering subgroup communication (ethnic, racial, social, economic).	———	———	———	———
b. smoothing the transition from childhood to adulthood.	———	———	———	———
c. fostering aspirations even if there is no pathway to them.	———	———	———	———
d. giving the student a number of roles, even if these roles are incompatible.	———	———	———	———
e. finding ways to meet basic organic needs of food and health.	———	———	———	———
f. promoting living styles consistent with the changing material base.	———	———	———	———

continued

	Strongly agree	Agree	Disagree	Strongly disagree
g. educating for mankind rather than serving national or local orientations.	_____	_____	_____	_____
h. creating experiences that show the real, not necessarily the ideal.	_____	_____	_____	_____

3. Types of knowledge that the school should encourage are:
   a. subjective, derived from one's perceptions, feelings, and senses. _____ _____ _____ _____
   b. subjective, derived from personal intuition. _____ _____ _____ _____
   c. objective, derived from reason. _____ _____ _____ _____
   d. derived from our cultural traditions. _____ _____ _____ _____

4. Characteristics of children that the school should recognize include:
   a. competence to make decisions about what they should learn. _____ _____ _____ _____
   b. natural tendencies that should be replaced with more acceptable ones. _____ _____ _____ _____

continued

104 — SELECTING AMONG EDUCATIONAL OBJECTIVES

		Strongly agree	Agree	Disagree	Strongly disagree
c.	a need to be shaped to desired outcomes rather than merely encouraged to reveal their inherent creativity.	_____	_____	_____	_____
d.	wide variations in mental development and potential.	_____	_____	_____	_____
e.	ability of all to achieve common objectives (although they require different amounts of time in order to achieve).	_____	_____	_____	_____
f.	ability of intelligence, attitudes, and motor behavior to be modified by instruction.	_____	_____	_____	_____
g.	a time (age) when something must be taught because it is unlikely to be learned at an older age.	_____	_____	_____	_____

Module 4

EVALUATING THE EFFECTIVENESS OF THE CURRICULUM

We have seen that evaluation plays an essential part in selecting learning opportunities, guiding responses to the data used in formulating educational objectives, and justifying objectives. Now we shall consider evaluation as it relates to the following three questions:

1. Are the learning activities in a given course or program accomplishing the desired outcomes (*summative evaluation*)? If not, which aspects need revising (*formative evaluation*)?
2. How can one best establish the validity of claims made by students of curriculum planning and hierarchical structures in curriculum design?
3. How can one best compare the effectiveness of different curricula?

OBJECTIVES OF THIS MODULE

The following competencies, which relate directly to the evaluation of learning activities, materials, and programs, can be acquired by reading the text material and completing the exercises:

1. The user will be able to differentiate among goals, activities, and objectives. The user will be able to infer and state measurable objectives consistent with given goals and activities.
2. The user will be able to contrast criterion-referenced and norm-referenced tests in terms of their underlying assumptions and manner of construction.
3. Given objectives, the user will be able to designate the most appropriate kind of measuring device to use for each objective (for example, self-report, checklist for observation of learner, checklist for observation of product, paper and pencil tests).

4. The user will be able to suggest multiple measures for evaluating learning activities, including unobtrusive measures and direct and indirect self-reports.
5. Given case studies involving different evaluation designs (for example, *randomized posttest only*), the user will be able to label each design and state its advantages and disadvantages.
6. Given various purposes for evaluating (for example, course improvement, validation of curricular hierarchies, assessment of outcomes), the user will be able to identify the role and procedure appropriate to each purpose.
7. Given data showing the results of evaluative studies in curriculum, the user will be able to interpret the data and draw warranted conclusions. The interpretations rest on knowledge of such statistical concepts as the confidence interval, reliability, and statistical and practical significance.

Instruments and Situations

Goals and educational and instructional objectives are the *ends* in view. Learning activities appropriate for achieving these ends are the *means* to be employed. The ends-means distinction is convenient when evaluating learning activities, but we should remember that values are tested by both their grounds and their consequences. Further, a value that is held as an end is always regarded as a means when it is in some larger frame of reference.

Most evaluators of learning activities first try to find out what purposes the learning activities are to serve, that is, what it is that the learner should know and be able to do as a consequence of the activities. Next, they attempt to collect evidence that indicates whether or not the desired changes occurred in the learner.

It is not feasible to collect such evidence, however, without first stating, in an operational or measurable manner, the changes sought. Purposes stated as broad goals (for example, citizenship, reading, health) delimit the area of measurement, but not enough. Also, goals are seldom if ever recorded because they encompass so many different dimensions. Goethe's comment in his eightieth year is a case in point: "The dear people do not know how long it takes to learn to read. I have been at it all my life, and I cannot say that I have reached the goal." The objectives of a single lesson, a unit of study, a course, or a program may all contribute to a single goal. Often, the curricular evaluator is given only broad goal statements and is expected to convert them to instructional objectives so that appropriate measures can be made. The evaluator does so only when he or she realizes that the objectives will seldom be equivalent to the goals. The best that can be hoped is that the objectives will be consistent with the ideal. An example of the relation between the goal and different levels of objectives appears below:

1. *Goal statement* The learner will exemplify good citizenship. This goal could guide an entire school program. However, there are at least 250 definitions of citizenship. Particular course objectives must be more specific in stating the aspect of citizenship to be advanced from the learning opportunities.
2. *Educational objective* The learner will be able to relate principles of civil rights to current events. Educational objectives are written at the level given in the *Taxonomy of Educational Objectives*.[1] This level is often appropriate for giving general directions for planning a course or program. It is not always specific enough for test construction.
3. *Instructional objective* Given newspaper accounts of persons involved in court trials, the learner will be able to state in writing what individual rights in each situation are and are not guaranteed according to the Constitution. This level approximates the specificity required for test construction. There is both a domain indicating the kind of stimuli that could be used for a test item (newspaper accounts of persons involved in court trials) and direction indicating the kind of observable response to be made by learner (a written constructed re-

---

1. Benjamin S. Bloom, ed., *Taxonomy of Educational Objectives* (New York: David McKay Company, 1956).

sponse). Further, there is a criterion of correctness, a way to tell what constitutes acceptable answers (definition of rights as found in the Constitution). An example of a test question that would be in accordance with this objective is: " 'Adams, the prisoner, said he wanted to compel several people to appear as witnesses and to question them.' Should both of these requests be granted? Why? Why not? Write your answer."

Exercise 1 *Differentiating among goals, objectives, activities*

First, put *A* by any statement that is an activity; *G* by any statement that is a goal, and *O* by any statement that is an objective. Second, change the activities and goals to objectives by modifying the original statements to include both a domain and an observable learner behavior (response). Write the objective below the original statement.

_____ 1. The student will develop skill in reading (mathematics, geography, etc.).

_____ 2. The student will be given pictures, recordings, and a "live" performance featuring various orchestral instruments.

112 — EVALUATING THE EFFECTIVENESS OF THE CURRICULUM

_____ 3. Given any Spanish *ar* verb, the student will be able to conjugate it in the present and imperfect tenses.

_____ 4. The student will be able to use the dictionary.

_____ 5. Given a sentence with a verb omitted, the student will select from two alternatives the word that will complete the sentence in the most descriptive manner. Example: The rain (pounded, fell) on the roof.

Answers

1. G   This goal could be changed to an objective by specifying a domain situation and observable learner response consistent with the goal. One objective might be: Given one-syllable words with regular spelling patterns and familiar initial consonants (domain), the learner will pronounce the word (observable response).
2. A   This statement could be changed to an objective by considering what might follow from such an activity. A domain is specified in these two examples: Given individual pictures of familiar musical instruments (stimuli), the learner will

be able to write the name of each instrument (response). Given taped sounds played by different familiar musical instruments (stimuli), the learner will identify each instrument by circling one of several pictures (response).
3. O This statement does not need to be changed.
4. G This goal could be changed by stating any of several domains of stimuli (guide words, diacritical markings, pronunciation rules, words not in alphabetical order, dictionary entries), and specifying "use" in terms of observable responses (list the words found, orally pronounce words, give the preferred pronunciations, give the origin of the word, divide the word).
5. O This statement does not need to be changed.

SPECIFICATIONS FOR CRITERION-REFERENCED TESTS

The essence of criterion-referenced measurement is that the measures are congruent with clearly stated objectives. An objective is clearly stated when it has been amplified to include these four elements:

1. The stimulus element of a domain is given. Example: all regular *ar*, *er*, and *ir* Spanish verbs (the content from which items can be drawn).
2. Directions given respondents indicate the overt responses to be made. Example: Look at each verb and the form desired (*yo, tu, usted*), and then *circle the answer* that corresponds to the imperfect tense for the verb and form.
3. The false responses (the distractors) are specified. Example: The false options will consist of verbs ending in the preterite and present tenses. There will be three options to each problem.

4. Criteria for correctness are given. Example: A correct answer will be in accordance with the Spanish declension for the imperfect tense. (Note: If a constructed response had been called for, one would have to stipulate whether or not spelling and accent marks were required for correctness.)

The presence of the above four elements makes it possible to design tests that measure pretty much what the objective calls for. The correspondence between test and objective is a prized quality of criterion-referenced testing.

Exercise 2 *Identifying features of an amplified objective*

Look at the elements of the amplified objective below and then indicate which of the following labels best describes each element.

a. stimulus   b. directions   c. response options
d. criterion for correctness

Objective: Student will be able to select from a list the word that contains a silent letter.

_____ 1. The population of silent letters to which the learner must respond are: *b* before a consonant (except *l* and *r*); *b* after *m*; *c* before *k*; *g* in *ght*; *g* before *n*; *k* before *n*; *l* after a consonant; *w* before *r*.

_____ 2. The student will be asked to circle each word on each line containing a letter that is not pronounced.

_____ 3. Three words will appear on a line. One or more of these words will contain silent letters. There will be five lines per page. Each of the three words will be of one or two syllables; all words will be drawn from the Dolch List of words frequently found in primary materials.

_____   4. The correct answer is the word containing a letter that is not pronounced according to the rules given in statement 1.

Answers

1. *a* The statement specifies the domain of letters to appear.
2. *b* Directions are given in the statement.
3. *c* The statement specifies the response options—it gives their number and characteristics.
4. *d* A rule is given for judging an answer correct or not.

NORM-REFERENCED TESTS

Norm-referenced tests, too, are planned in accordance with specifications. Each item is supposed to contain an important concept, and the difficulty of an item is intended to be based on reasoning or knowledge rather than esoteric subject matter. Distractors are written with as much care as the correct answer. (A distractor may be a common misconception, a statement that is true but doesn't satisfy the requirements of the problem, or something that may appear plausible to the uninformed.) The essential characteristic of norm-referenced tests, however, is their *response variance*. Typically, questions that can be answered correctly by 90 percent or more of the students or by fewer than 10 percent are not considered useful enough to include in the test. Norm-referenced tests are designed to permit comparison between an individual's performance and that of a norm group, hence the tests must use items that elicit a wide range of test scores.

Norm-referenced tests are not useful for judging the effectiveness of curricular offerings because they seldom measure what is taught. In order to get variance among respondents, items that reflect what is best taught (that which most pupils learn) must be eliminated. The result is a test that functions like an intelligence test—it is far less susceptible to change through instruction than criterion-referenced tests, which match the objectives of the program. Therefore, when we are interested in measuring treatment effect, we must not use norm-referenced standardized achievement tests that are really aptitude tests. Aptitude tests are supposed to predict the future performance of individuals as compared to an average individual performing the tasks. A test constructed to maximize discriminating power emphasizes aptitude and deemphasizes achievement.

Exercise 3 *Contrasting criterion-referenced and norm-referenced tests*

Indicate which kind of test best fits each description.

a. criterion-referenced test
b. norm-referenced test

_____ 1. Better for comparing individuals and groups

_____ 2. Better for diagnosing particular strengths and weaknesses of learner

_____ 3. Better for determining whether an instructional technique was effective

_____ 4. Better for assessing the effects of particular curricular material

_____ 5. More likely to reveal pretest and posttest growth

_____ 6. More likely to deal with large content area (more global objectives)

_____ 7. Allows learners to achieve mastery

_____ 8. More likely to match the instructional program

_____ 9. More likely to provide evidence regarding attainment of all the teacher's objectives

_____ 10. Has more items for assessing a learner's competency in a given task

Answers

1. *b* A norm-referenced test "spreads" students out.
2. *a* This test helps identify specific objectives that haven't been met. Even the subtests of norm-referenced tests measure broad areas of ability rather than the highly specific components that can lead to direct remedial efforts.
3. *a* A criterion-referenced test is sensitive to instruction.
4. *a* A criterion-referenced test allows matching of objectives, materials, and tests.
5. *a* Competency is measured more than aptitude; learning activities affect learner's competencies more than their aptitudes.
6. *b* Norm-referenced tests tend to contain difficult vocabulary and require inferences that are not critical to mastery of the concepts and principles being tested.
7. *a* A criterion-referenced test measures the skill, competence, and knowledge that are achievable, although not all learners will achieve at the same time or rate.
8. *a* Objective-based tests can be selected for their agreement with the program.
9. *a* There can be as many separate tests as objectives.
10. *a* Such tests typically have several items for each objective, thereby increasing their reliability.

ALTERNATIVES TO PAPER AND PENCIL TESTS

In one sense any set of systematic observations used to measure human behavior is a test. Structured interviews and other direct observational techniques, for example, are tests. Most people, however, think of multiple-choice, essay, and constructed response measures—using pencil and paper—as tests.

Curricular evaluators must use something more than paper and pencil tests in their efforts to assess the effects of learning activities, courses, and programs. This is so because (1) it is a good idea to use more than one instrument for establishing the validity of the program and tapping different dimensions of the objective (this is called a *triangulation* strategy in measurement); (2) paper and pencil tests may not reveal what a learner has achieved, and they are often unfair and not valid measures for culturally different learners; and (3) some objectives are more accurately and economically measured by techniques other than paper and pencil tests.

THREE USEFUL TECHNIQUES

1. One way of evaluating the effectiveness of an activity or program is through observation of learner products such as painting, compositions, or construction. The observation should, however, be guided by a checklist specifying the qualities that would indicate success. For example, paintings should show harsh and soft lines, balanced contrast, reciprocal use of negative and positive space, and uniqueness; compositions should show colorful words, variety in types of sentences, and appropriate use of passive and active voice.

2. A curricular evaluator may also observe the learner in given situations—conducting an experiment, solving a problem, participating in a discussion, performing a dance. These observations, too, should be undertaken using a checklist stipulating the behavior that should be exhibited (order or sequence, specific physical movements, particular learning strategies, choices, and adherence to given conventions).
3. Attitudes, appreciations, feelings, preferences, and the like are often best indicated by self-reports, the responses the learner gives in oral interviews and questionnaires.

Exercise 4 *Relating types of measures to general goals*

Look at each goal and indicate the best type of measure to use with that goal.

a. checklist for product   b. paper and pencil test
c. self-report   d. checklist for observation of learner

_____ 1. The child will be able to follow the sequence of instructions.

_____ 2. The child's paintings will display more artistic qualities, such as uniqueness.

_____ 3. The child will use a particular method in setting up his experiments or solving problems.

_____ 4. The child will be able to solve problems.

_____ 5. The child will read orally with proper inflection.

_____ 6. The child will be able to recognize the tone and mood set by the author.

_____ 7. The child will read different kinds of books (types of literature).

_____ 8. The child will take part in group discussions.

_____ 9. The child will take his turn.

_____ 10. When at home, the child will do his homework before watching TV.

Answers

1. *d* Observation is best, although the existence of a product or a right answer might also indicate that instructions were followed.
2. *a* The product will reveal the presence or absence of the desired quality.
3. *d* Observation will reveal the method the child used.
4. *b* A paper and pencil test is most economical, although the product is another indicator. If one wanted to know how a student solved the problem, an observation would be best.
5. *d* Observation of the child reading aloud is the best way to monitor inflection.
6. *b* A paper and pencil test is best, but one could ask the learner to give a self-report about the author's tone and mood.
7. *d* Observation and self-report, perhaps using a questionnaire or inventory, are both good indicators.
8. *d* Observation of the child's participation will reveal attainment of this goal.
9. *d* Observation to note whether the child takes his turn is the most appropriate measure.
10. *c* A self-report is best, but a parent might use observation.

EVIDENCE OF EXISTING RECORDS

Inferences about program effectiveness can be made unobtrusively without demanding learner cooperation (nonobtrusive). School records themselves can be quantified to reveal changes in learner motivation, attitude, and knowledge. Examples of settings for making such measures are:

1. *The library* number and kind of books withdrawn; descriptions of pupils withdrawing books voluntarily
2. *The attendance office* absences, tardiness
3. *The nurse's office* nature and kinds of accidents, illnesses
4. *The cafeteria* food choices, seating patterns (cross-age, ethnic groupings)
5. *The administrator's and counselor's offices* number and kinds of critical incidents reflecting quantifiable categories of behavior; number of withdrawals from particular classes; the extent of pupil participation in specified school social activities

DIRECT AND INDIRECT SELF-REPORTS

The assessment of personality and affect is thought to be more susceptible to faking than the assessment of cognitive behavior. Also, learners may sometimes not feel free to reveal their true beliefs. Hence, two measurement provisions are made:

1. *Anonymity* Learners are asked to make anonymous self-reports through questionnaires. Even little children can circle one of five distinguishing faces to reveal how they feel about

something or someone. The assessor need not know how each individual responds. The consequences of a particular learning experience need not pertain only to the individual learner; they may pertain to a whole population of learners. During some kinds of instruction, of course, the teacher may want to monitor the responses of each individual.

2. *Camouflage* A teacher may discover the learner's true disposition by camouflaging or masking the instrument's true purpose or observing learners without letting them know they are being observed. In these days of increased sensitivity to the ethics of privacy, evaluators should at least be sure that no learner will be harmed in any way and that the assessment is warranted because the results are likely to lead to better experiences for a number of learners.

The exercise to follow will clarify the distinctions among (1) a *direct self-report* (in which the learner can guess what the questioner is trying to find out); (2) an *indirect self-report* (in which the intent of the questioner is camouflaged, or the desired right answer is not readily apparent to the learner); and (3) an *observational indicator*—a situation (either contrived or natural) that allows an observer to get evidence indicating what learners might have acquired from particular learning activities, a course, or a program.

First, however, it should be pointed out that an indirect self-report often includes items of *high inference*. High inference means that the assessor infers from the learner's responses that a particular belief is held rather than measuring that belief directly. For example, it is believed that learners as a group have lower self-concepts when they do not like their own names. Hence, in reviewing responses to an instrument that asks learners to write three names they like and three names they dislike, the evaluator infers that those who dislike their names have lower self-concepts.

Exercise 5 *Identifying self-reports (direct and indirect) and observational indicators*

Label each measure as:

a. direct self-report   b. indirect self-report
c. observational indicator

_____ 1. As a measure of his attitude toward school subjects, a student is asked to state how much he would pay for each autograph of a number of listed persons. Persons include those from the fields of arts, sports, religion, sciences, and the like.

_____ 2. As a measure of attitude toward what was taught in a music course, sales reports from a local music store are sorted by type of music.

_____ 3. As a measure of her attitude toward her peers, a pupil is asked to name the pupils who would be chosen by the teacher for certain activities in the classroom and also to name those she would choose for these opportunities.

_____ 4. As a measure of attitude toward learning, time samplings are made of writings on desks, including those categorized as "doodles" and "cribs."

_____ 5. As a measure of his attitude toward himself, the pupil is asked to respond to statements such as: friends usually follow my ideas; older kids do not like me; I wish I were younger; I am a cheerful person.

6. As a measure of his attitude toward himself, a child is asked to say which roles he would be willing to play in a show. Roles depict positions of high and low status. The greater number of roles selected is assumed to indicate a higher self-concept.

7. As a measure of Chicano integration in a school, counts are made of such things as the number of articles in the school paper written in Spanish, cluster groupings during free play, and membership in voluntary school organizations.

Answers

1. *b* (*indirect self-report*)   The learner is unlikely to know his attitude toward school subjects is being assessed.
2. *c* (*observational indicator*)   Sales of the type of music featured in the course would have increased if the teacher had been successful.
3. *a* (*direct self-report*)   The child is giving a direct report regarding how she feels about her peers.
4. *c* (*observational indicator*)   Writings on desks can reveal interests or such states as boredom and anxiety.
5. *a* (*direct self-report*)   The learner could easily recognize that he is being asked to make a self-assessment.
6. *b* (*indirect self-report*)   The learner does not know that willingness to play unfavorable roles indicates a high self-concept.
7. *c* (*observational indicator*)   An increased number of articles in Spanish and voluntary associations indicate progress toward integration.

DESCRIPTIONS OF PUBLISHED TEST INSTRUMENTS

There are several sources that both list and evaluate test instruments. The Social Science Education Consortium, 855 Broadway, Boulder, Colorado 80302, for example, has analyzed and catalogued a thousand social studies evaluative instruments. The Center for the Study of Evaluation, UCLA, 405 Hilgard, Los Angeles, California 90024, has four publications that describe and evaluate thousands of elementary school tests, preschool and kindergarten tests, tests for higher order cognitive, affective, and interpersonal skills, and secondary school tests. Many measures of social psychological attitudes are available in a publication by John Robinson and Phillip Stover of the Survey Research Center Institute for Social Research at the University of Michigan. O. K. Buro's *Sixth Mental Measurements Yearbook* (Highland Park, N.J.: Gryphon Press, 1965) is another source for those who want to review tests in print.

EVALUATION DESIGNS

Thus far we have focused on instruments for collecting information that will indicate whether the purposes of learning activities, courses, and programs are achieved. Now we will consider some of the most common designs or procedures for collecting the data.

When one wants to attribute any change in the learners to a given program, one must administer the measures both at the beginning and at the end of the program. This is a *pretest-posttest design*. In order to show, however, that any changes are due to the program and not to maturation of learners or some other experiences that are going on at the time, it is sometimes possible to administer the same tests to students who were not in the program. When a control group is added to the original design, there is a *pretest-posttest control group design.* If those who were in the program change their behaviors and perceptions and the others don't, one may assume that the program was responsible.

One difficulty with using a control group is that learners serving as the control may be quite different (for example, more highly motivated, or brighter) from the experimental group. Hence, some evaluators try to compare only those members of the two groups who share common attributes, such as grade point averages and scholastic aptitudes.

A more useful design, however, is the *randomized posttest only control.* In this procedure, learners are randomly assigned to two different groups (using a toss of a coin, every other name on the roll book, or a table of random numbers) and both groups receive the same posttest although only one group is given the program. Differences found constitute evidence for or against the program. The *randomized posttest only control design* is also useful when the evaluator wishes to compare the effects of different programs.

A fourth design is called the *interrupted time series design.* This design is useful for studying longitudinal effects and for evaluating curricular intervention when there are comparison groups. The design consists of a series of measurements both before and after the introduction of the intervention. Any noticeable change in the series of measurements at the time of the intervention and afterwards may be attributed to the intervention, as shown below.

Indicator of Achievement Level

	Week 1	Week 2	Week 3	Week 4	Week 5	Week 6
Group A	−	−	−	+*	+	+
Group B	−	−	−	−	−	−

*The intervention is introduced to Group A during the fourth week.

Exercise 6 *Recognizing evaluation designs*

Read each situation and then indicate, in the space provided, which design was used.

_____ 1. A school has daily attendance records for a population of pupils. The staff thought that by introducing an alternative activity day, in which pupils would pursue studies of their interest, the pupils' attitudes toward school as measured by attendance would improve. Measures show that not only did pupils attend more frequently on activity day but on subsequent days as well.
   a. pretest-posttest
   b. posttest only control
   c. interrupted time series

_____ 2. A teacher is asked to evaluate the effect of two textbooks on the attitudes of pupils toward Mexicans. One textbook presents much factual data about Mexican culture; the other is more narrative and biographical, featuring characters with whom the learners can identify. The teacher randomly assigns pupils to one or the other of the two books and at the end of the unit collects anonymous attitude measures from pupils in each group. The scores of the two groups are contrasted even though individuals responding are not identified.
   a. control group design
   b. randomized posttest only control
   c. interrupted time series

3. Prior to the introduction of a new reading series, pupils were tested on several measures such as comprehension skills, word attack skills, and motives for reading. Subsequently, only certain classrooms received and used the new series. Pupils in classrooms with and without the new reading series were then given a number of posttests.
   a. pretest-posttest
   b. pretest-posttest control group
   c. randomized pretest only control

4. During a school's needs assessment, a number of pupils were identified as feeling powerless on the basis of responses to a locus of control measure. Subsequently, these pupils were given a special program that focused on helping them accept responsibility, when warranted, for both their accomplishments and their disappointments. The same locus of control test was administered to the pupils at the conclusion of the program.
   a. pretest-posttest
   b. pretest-posttest control group
   c. interrupted time series

Answers

1. *c* (*interrupted time series*)   A series is present within which the effect of the innovation can be noted.
2. *b* (*randomized posttest only control*)   Pupils are randomly assigned to treatment.
3. *b* (*pretest-posttest control group*)   The effects of two treatments are noted by pretest-posttest gains.
4. *a* (*pretest-posttest*)   Pretest-posttest gains are noted for a single group of pupils.

Design
and Decisions

Evaluators speak of *summative* evaluation, which is the assessment of programs or materials on the basis of their overall effects. Summative evaluation is useful in making decisions regarding which of several programs or materials is better than others. This kind of evaluation requires finding out both whether, say, a particular set of materials produces the effect promised and what happens to learners with respect to other objectives. In short, summative evaluation means looking for likely side effects (prejudices, alienations, self-depreciation), and getting evidence of learner change on a wide range of objectives. Parenthetically, when this has been done, it is usually found that innovative curricula are not superior to traditional curricula. Each curriculum seems to do better on the distinctive parts of its own program and about equal on the parts they have in common.

Formative evaluation takes place when the evaluator collects information in order to decide how to improve the program or material. The formative evaluator is mostly interested in a product, material, or program that achieves particular outcomes, not all the objectives that any consumer might want. In order to achieve these limited objectives, several strategies are employed:

1. The entire program is tried out with a sample of the intended learner population. Posttest results indicate which of the objectives have been reached. Any objectives not reached indicate deficiencies in the program, which must be corrected.
2. Segments of the program are used with representative learners of the intended population. Each segment is responsible for the achievement of an *en route objective*. Only if posttests of the en route objective are mastered, is the segment considered satisfactory. Unsuccessful scores pinpoint aspects that must be modified.
3. Segments of the program are tried out with individual learners. The responses and comments of these learners are monitored to reveal aspects that interfered with the learner's successful performance.

When one must decide on the validity of hierarchical structures in an instructional sequence, several approaches are used:

1. Learners who demonstrate mastery of a "terminal" objective are asked to take tests that measure en route objectives. Any en route objective that is not mastered is likely to be a "false" prerequisite.
2. A group of learners who cannot perform the terminal and en route objectives are randomly assigned to experimental and control groups. Only the experimental group is given a program leading to achievement of the en route objectives. Later both groups receive instruction on the terminal task to reveal the effects of the prerequisite instruction.

Matrix sampling is an evaluative technique of great value when decisions are to be made about the program as opposed to decisions about individual learners. In this procedure, individuals within a group (classroom, school, or district) receive different test items or different criterion-referenced tests. Matrix sampling is a combination of item sampling and examinee sampling. The results reflect the effect of the program on the group but not on any one individual. The advantages of this technique are many. One advantage is that many objectives can be assessed. If, for example, a teacher has thirty objectives and thirty pupils, with matrix sampling each pupil might complete only three or five tests, each test measuring a different objective. Only a sample of the pupils would indicate the program's effect on each objective, but data on each objective would be collected—something that would be very difficult to do if each pupil had to complete thirty tests. In addition to the economy in testing time and materials, matrix sampling can be an advantage in that learners feel less intimidated when given tests or items that are different from those given most of their peers. They know that they can't be compared when they are not being measured by the same instrument.

Exercise 7 *Relating purpose to roles and procedures*

Indicate which procedure is most appropriate for each purpose.

_____ 1. To diagnose an individual learner's strength and weakness in a given area
   a. use matrix sampling.
   b. use individual testing.

_____ 2. To choose among different curricular materials
   a. use formative evaluation.
   b. use summative evaluation.

_____ 3. To improve a course of study
   a. use formative evaluation.
   b. use summative evaluation.

132—EVALUATING THE EFFECTIVENESS OF THE CURRICULUM

_____ 4. To validate a hierarchical curricular structure
   a. scramble the order of objectives.
   b. seek multiple side effects.

_____ 5. To assess many kinds of outcomes from a given program
   a. use matrix sampling.
   b. give all learners the same test(s).

Answers

1. b The focus is on the individual.
2. b Products are compared.
3. a Formative evaluation provides information useful in revising a particular course.
4. a There is no hierarchy if objectives can be acquired in any order.
5. a Matrix sampling allows for more objectives to be measured. When all learners take the same test(s), time and fatigue preclude the measuring of large numbers of objectives.

INTERPRETING MEASURES OF CHANGE

Typically, scores generated by assessment measures are: (1) compared with what is called for in the objective to indicate success or deficiency, (2) compared by groups (control and experimental) to reveal the significance of differences between means and proportions in order to show the relative effects of the different activities or programs, or (3) correlated with each other to indicate relations among the different measures. By statistical procedures we can determine whether the changes and different scores are true changes or chance occurrences. Statistical tests are more likely to indicate a change as true when there is a large mean (average) difference between two sets of scores, a large sample size, and small variability in one of the sets of scores. However, it is not enough for the curriculum worker to know the *statistical significance* of the findings. Thought must be given to their *practical significance*, the importance of the finding for making decisions about adopting, modifying, or eliminating aspects of the learning activities, course, program, and the like.

Practical significance means questioning, for example, whether a difference of three, five, ten, or more points on certain measures—albeit statistically significant—justifies a basis for action. (The importance of even a few points' difference under some circumstances can be seen by recalling that businesses can go bankrupt over the loss of a few percentage points.)

One way to help decide on the practical importance of the results is to be sure about the findings. There are several ways to verify one's findings:

1. An evaluator can verify the true magnitude of a reported difference through a statistical calculation called a *confidence interval*. The confidence interval indicates the probability that the same results would be retained if the evaluation study were replicated.
2. One can determine that the association between a particular curricular package (textbook, intervention, activity, course, or program) and the outcome measure is so close that one can predict the outcome knowing the particular curricular aspect.
3. An evaluator may show that multiple measures of the same outcome generally give similar results. This is a test of *validity*.
4. An evaluator may offer some evidence that the learners' responses were stable. Two sets of learner responses to the same measure, for example, should show agreement. This is a test of *reliability*.

Exercise 8   *Interpreting findings*

Read each situation and then indicate the best answer in the space provided.

_____ 1. Results of a study comparing intervention *A* with intervention *B* show that learners using *A* averaged ten points more achievement on an outcome measure. A confidence interval for this observed difference indicates that there is a 95 percent chance that replications would place the true difference somewhere between eight and twelve points. The evaluator should conclude that:
   a. *A* is a more effective intervention.
   b. no reliable difference exists.

_____ 2. The correlation between the use of one set of materials by 100 learners and an outcome measure is .30. The probability that this is a true finding is quite high, $p < .05$. A correlation of .30 indicates that 91 percent of the variance cannot be accounted for by the materials. One only has to square the correlation and subtract from 100 to estimate the variance accounted for. For example: $(.3)^2 = .09 = 9/100 = 9\%$. The evaluator should conclude that the materials:
   a. are not a factor in the learner's achievement.
   b. are influencing learners.

_____ 3. Results of an effort to reduce prejudice show that students in an experimental antiprejudice program showed a 10 percent increase in their prejudice (as measured by a pre- and post-prejudice indicator) at the end of the program. A control group that received no instruction in this area increased their prejudice by 30 percent during the same period. A statistical test shows the probability of this event's being chance occurs in less than 5 times in 100 ($p < .05$). The evaluator should conclude that:
   a. the experimental program had a positive influence.
   b. neither program showed a significant difference in progress toward the goal.

_____ 4. Results of an effort to improve self-concepts have shown change, but the three measures used have low reliability. When each measure was administered a second time without intervening instruction, the correlations were only .25, .26, and .30 respectively. The correlation among the measures, however, is quite high: .60. The evaluator should conclude that:
   a. the tests are too unreliable to be used in drawing conclusions.
   b. the congruency among the measures indicates that the measures are valid (they are measuring a common definition of self-concept).

Answers

1. *a* The confidence interval suggests that the difference is a true difference and not a chance occurrence.
2. *b* The use of the materials is influencing learners although other influences are greater.
3. *a* The experimental program is positive in that it prevented prejudices from increasing to a greater extent than the pro-

gram giving no attention to the problem. Obviously, however, the goal of eliminating prejudices has not been achieved.

4. *b* A correlation of .60 indicates that the three measures are measuring a common attribute. Low reliability in self-concept measures may be due to the fact that learners fluctuate in this dimension. Although individual predictions cannot be made on the basis of such low reliability measures, predictions for a group are in order.

Practical significance is also found by weighing the costs of attending and not attending to the findings. One might ask: What values will be given up if one course of action is followed rather than another? What will be involved in trying to rectify the deficiencies? What data do we have or can we get to show that teachers used the material as intended? What factors led learners to perceive their peers in unfavorable lights? What resources are required to act on the findings?

In short, the results demand further inquiry and call for both facts and value judgments, casting the participants into the evaluative roles treated in previous modules—deriving objectives, making defensible choices, and planning learning activities.

Summary

In order to summarize your own views about desirable practices in curriculum evaluation, please do the following:

First, consider a situation familiar to you that calls for evaluating an aspect of curriculum. (You may want to assess particular learning activities or materials, for example.)

Next, indicate below the evaluative procedures that you consider most appropriate for the situation.

_____ 1. Purpose for the evaluation
   a. formative evaluation (for example, improvement of materials or activity)
   b. summative evaluation (for example, comparison of programs or materials)
   c. validation of a curriculum hierarchy for ordering of activities or content

_____ 2. Level of generality to be treated in the evaluation
   a. goal statement
   b. educational objective
   c. instructional objective
   d. instructional activity

138 — EVALUATING THE EFFECTIVENESS OF THE CURRICULUM

    3. Instruments to be used
        a. published instruments
        b. locally developed instruments
        c. norm-referenced tests
        d. criterion-referenced tests
        e. direct self-reports
        f. indirect self-reports
        g. checklists for observation of learners
        h. unobtrusive records

    4. Special considerations
        a. use of triangulation
        b. amplified objectives to guide test writers

    5. Procedures to be followed
        a. pretest-posttest design
        b. pretest-posttest control group design
        c. randomized posttest only control
        d. interrupted time series design
        e. matrix sampling

    6. Interpretation (Which of the following will you determine?)
        a. statistical significance
        b. practical significance
        c. confidence intervals
        d. validity
        e. reliability